THE GREAT TROUSER MYSTERY

Graham Parker

Illustrated by Willy Smax

A Stiff Records Book

A Stiff Records Book
27 Alexander St., London W.2.
Published in 1980

Colouring by Karen Ludlow and Willy Smax

Typesetting by Yale Press Ltd, London, SE25

Printed in Great Britain by Caledonian Graphics Ltd.
and bound by Hunter & Foulis Ltd.

ISBN 0 427 00447 0

Contents

Chapter 1
A Remarkably Smarmy Pair

'Left Cerebrum pads.'

'Right cerebrum pads. RIGHT CEREBRUM PADS, LOVE!'

'Oh sorry, Dolse . . . whoops, nearly dozed off then!'

'Lobal vibes, ta Dilly. Have a hard night, did ya love? Been on the tickle with that boy o' ours eh?'

'Oh Dolse, no such luck mate, I'm just not with it today.'

Dilly giggled as she passed the two white, cone-shaped lobal pads to Dolse who placed them carefully on the sleeping patient's forehead.

'This one's a right one, isn't he love?' said Dolse.

Dolse was in her early thirties and had once been married, but she forgot about it some years ago. She had a ferrety face and black and purple hair which used to leave a mark on the wall in the canteen when she had tea.

'Is this the chap who's going out on a 7 a/w guitar tone?' asked Dilly, still slightly dazed. She was twenty-one and plumpish and had worked with Dolse for five years. Five years too long she sometimes thought, whenever it got too much. Dil and Dolse were very close.

'Yes mate, he must be in a right state, oohoo,' answered Dolse. 'Got a nice bump there 'asn't he? Look at that, Dil, I bet he's a bit hectic, this one!' Dolse gave Dil a nudge and a knowing wink. They both giggled and touched each other like children.

Dolse continued, 'We'll leave matey here on for an hour, and have a nice cuppa and a slab of soya bread, leave him to iron out the old brain cells, eh mate!'

'Yeah mate, I hope it'll be the last time this week. How many times has he been in here Dolse, at least three sessions in the last two days, isn't it?'

They slipped out of the room keeping very near to each other. The door closed behind them as they walked off along the echoing corridor, chattering inanely, leaving the patient plastered with cerebrum pads and lobal vibes, internally melting out the frictions with guitar power, his own favourite medicine.

'Good morning, Mr Tablet, nice day,' said Dolse and Dil simultaneously as they daintily slipped into a bubble chair at the end of the corridor.

'Wha . . . oh yeah, hallo girls, zooming! Ready for the downer then?'

'Oooo, goin' down together then are we?' gurgled Dil.

'Why not?' Mr Tablet gave them a smile and pressed the button at the side of the bubble chair he was sitting in and Dolse did the same with theirs. The girls always sat in the same chair when going down the escalator to the tea room, even though these were only single ones. They didn't like being separated, although young Dil occasionally yearned for a ride down on her own.

There was a slight whirring sound as the bubbles slid down to the canteen and Mr Tablet jumped out with his usual vigour; the girls however managed to get stuck.

They looked just like two rats in their brown lab coats, laughing gleefully, wedged in the perspex bubble.

Two rats in a hole, thought Mr Tablet, who was laughing a different kind of laugh than the girls. He spun on his heel looking very efficient but feeling a mess inside. 'Stimp, I've got to help these two pankers out again, why didn't I go down faster?' thought Mr Tablet, as he put his arm inside the opening of the bubble chair and around plump Dilly. He had to twist her around the bubble and out backwards, he was almost touching her left breast and was thinking how he'd like to have her across one of the music therapy couches, if he ever had the chance. Impossible, he realised, no way could you separate her from that old bitch, Dolse. A right couple of drivellers they were. 'There we are, ladies, all right now, we hope?'

They both giggled, said ta, and walked off to find their usual seat by the window. Mr Tablet was looking at Dil's back and imagining the big bum under that dull brown lab coat.

'Hmm.'

The happy couple sat in the tattered twentieth-century seats looking at each other across the table. the metal framed seats looked so incongruous in the plush canteen with its velvet upholstery and abstract mosaic walls. They pressed two buttons on a panel sunk into the wall and immediately a chute slipped out and two perspex plates with soya bread scuttled down onto the table followed closely by two small silver flasks of tea.

'It's nice to sit down and rest the ole feet, isn't it, mate? – all that leaning about,' said Dolse. She spoke with what might have been called a slight country accent in years gone by, nowadays it was just peculiar.

'Cor yeah,' Dil said, and accidentally brushed knees with Dolse under the table. Dolse picked up her soya bread and nibbled it with a slightly shy, self-conscious look about her.

They talked mainly about their work. They were music therapy attendants, working in the greatest company business the world had ever known. The Music Therapy business.

After the workers' uprising of 1984, mental health in the civilised countries had slipped into very doubtful straits; it wasn't the cause, it wasn't even the key. Perhaps it was the trigger.

Music Therapy was a great discovery and appeared almost magically at just the right time. It was a tightly controlled medical service when it first began, used carefully and for the general well-being of the public; now, like most things, the control had slipped. The man who had first used Music Therapy and created the early prototype was upheld by many as a saint, by others as a devil. Some admitted his genius but called him a clown, a buffoon. Whatever, something in this brilliant but rotund human being had found the necessary requirements for survival. When everybody else was trying desperately to keep

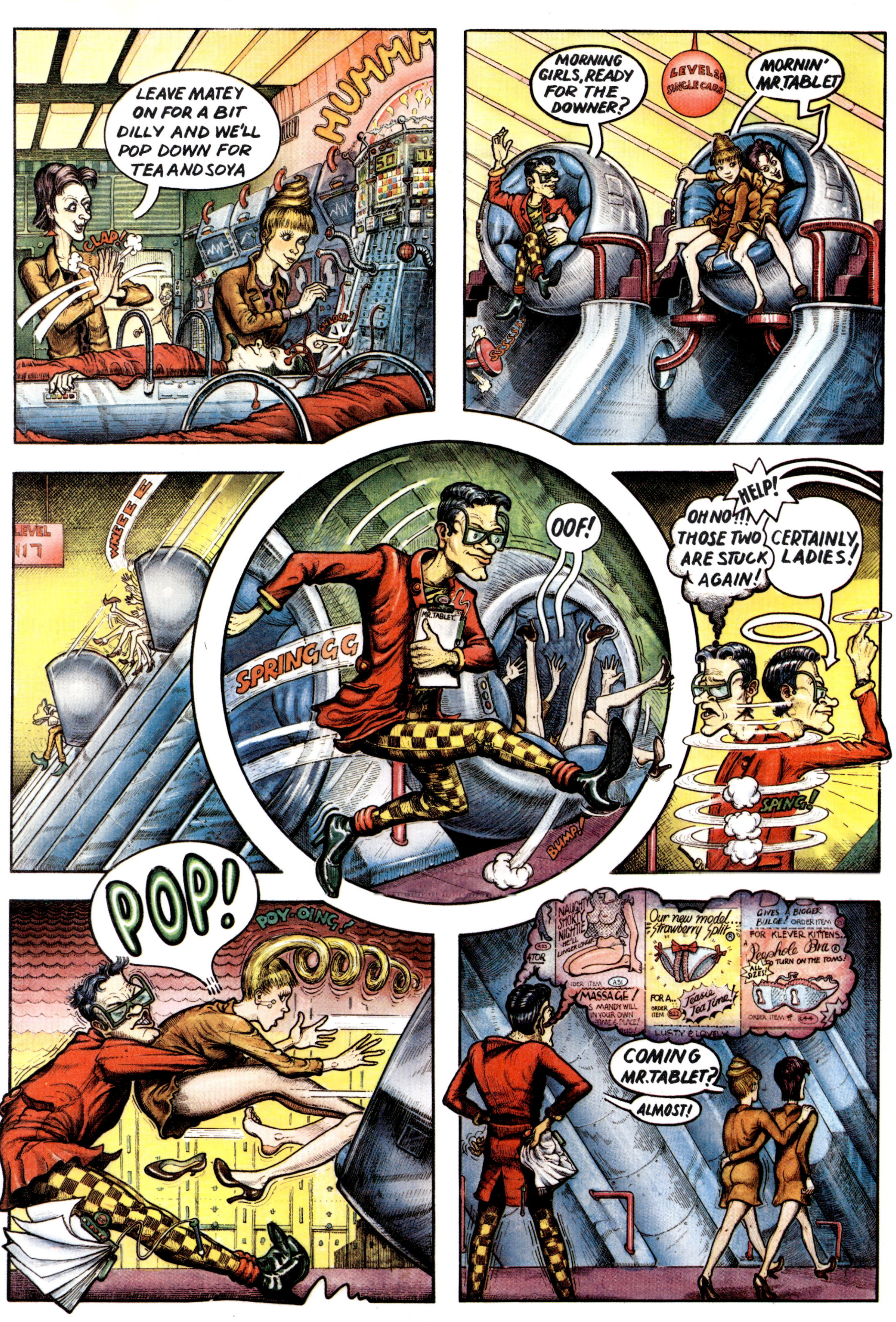
LEAVE MATEY ON FOR A BIT DILLY AND WE'LL POP DOWN FOR TEA AND SOYA
HUMMM
CLAP!
MORNING GIRLS, READY FOR THE DOWNER?
LEVEL 20 SINGLE CARS
MORNIN' MR.TABLET
SSSSSS
LEVEL 17
WHEEEE
OOF!
SPRINGGG
MR.TABLET
BUMP!
HELP!
OH NO!!! THOSE TWO ARE STUCK AGAIN!
CERTAINLY LADIES!
SPING!
POP!
POY-OING!
NAUGHTY SHORTY NIGHTIE HE'LL LINGER LONGER
ORDER ITEM A31
MASSAGE!
S MANDY WILL IN YOUR OWN TIME & PLACE!
Our new model... Strawberry Split ®
FOR A.. Teasie Tea Time!
ORDER ITEM B22
LUSTY & LOVELY
GIVES A BIGGER BULGE! ORDER ITEM
FOR KLEVER KITTENS..
A Peephole Bra ® TO TURN ON THE TOMS!
ALL SIZES!
ORDER ITEM # C44
COMING MR.TABLET?
ALMOST!

their heads above water, he went under it. Emerging not completely untouched, but with the answer that would ring in everyone's ears from now on – sound.

The man who founded, created, and made a vast fortune from the business, was one Mr T.G. Trouser.

Trouser. The peacemaker. Saviour. Squanderer. Mystic. Buffoon. Trouser the great leader whose lemmings would rush to the cliffs with the vibrations of a million instruments still trapped in their cells. Trouser, the electric Jesus.

He was not to be underestimated, as many of his adversaries had discovered, and he did have opponents. There were gangs of renegades in the city continually plotting his downfall, people without a purpose, who would kill for whoever paid the highest price. The highest price at the moment was being offered by two young men who had had power before Music Therapy. They had been in the artificial organ business but with Music Therapy curing the world's ailments, both were now rendered obsolete, a position they found most distasteful.

They were Jerry Can and Toni the Cortina. Gangsters extraordinary.

'And I'll tell you another thing Dil,' said Dolse, leaning over the old fashioned table towards Dil as if disclosing a vital secret, 'I reckon old Trouser's getting fed up with this business, I reckon he's after something else.' She was almost whispering in the quiet canteen, empty but for Mr Tablet who sat as far away from the pair as possible. 'I reckon 'e's got a rabbit up his stiff sleeve, maybe.'

Dil's eyes opened with a start at this comment and she choked on her bread; she'd heard Dolse talk in riddles before but it never ceased to amaze her how Dolse seemed so unaware of it and projected an air of absolute seriousness.

' 'E's out there now. . . Twiddling fate's knobs.' She spoke the words very slowly and deliberately, her black eyebrows lifting her eyeballs wider until Dil thought they would drop out in her tea.

'Uh yes . . . well mate, I think we'd better be getting back up top, Dolse mate, alright?'

'Yeah,' said Dolse as they left the table.

Dilly took her up in a bubble chair and put her on a couch with some low frequency organ music to put her together again. The attacks were frequent but not serious. She was good at her job.

Chapter 2
A Smelly Beginning

Against the sick green sky, streaked with blue lightning, a tattered silhouette could be seen, dragging itself along like a piece of animated seaweed.

Mr Straightly strained his eyes through the rain, holding his right hand above his eyebrows, as if it would help his vision, while his left hand gripped the door of his orange Range Rover to keep his balance in the wind. Mr Straightly was an Englishman in a time warp. A baffled man. This was probably his most baffled moment. He could not imagine why anyone should be out here in this dreadful weather on the border between Nepal and Tibet, without transport and running from the North where only cold mountains stood.

'Gad,' thought Mr Straightly.

He'd just been trekking through India reliving his ancestral past, but the world had changed and India was another place now. He wished he'd been his father. That was the era to live in. A man had power then; we're all sightseers now, he thought. . .absently.

The man came closer, dripping through the storm with flailing arms and Straightly could hear an English voice calling for help. After the initial shock he regained his senses and ran across the difficult terrain to the muddy figure's assistance.

'I say, old chap, are you in some sort of trouble there? Where on earth have you come from?' Mr Straightly, embarrassed that he'd never met this kind of situation before, put an arm around the figure and shoved him into the Range Rover. As he did so, he slipped in the mud and hit his face on the man's foot which was still dangling out of the door.

'Pank! Bally nuisance, wish I'd never come to this hellhole in the first place. Oh. . . Ah, excuse me. . .no offence meant. . . ah, I say, are you alright, man? Gad, I'm in a bally mess now, muck and slime.'

He slithered around to the other door, wet and sticky in khaki shorts, white hunter's hat and prawn moustache, and jumped in daintily, trying not to get the seat wet – as if it were possible.

The thunder cracked.

He wished he'd never noticed the man in the first place now. He'd only just picked up his outline rounding the bend in the track and had a curious feeling he should stop and see if it was really a man or his imagination. He felt something important would come of it if it was a man, out here, on the border of nowhere.

He was probably in his thirties; tubby build, golden-haired and dressed in a long robe with a raincoat over the top. His skin was strangely bright, healthy and flushed. He looked as if he'd been out in an English summer, sitting under apple trees, and not in the turbulence of Tibet.

He also stank.

It was a smell Mr Straightly could not identify. It had a definite atmosphere about it, similar to strong incense but even more elusive.

The lighting in the Range Rover made it seem like a capsule deep in a stormy sea. The stranger's features were highlighted occasionally by flashes of lightning; he was smiling contentedly, like a happy baby. After a moment or two he burst into what seemed to be a religious chant in a stilted foreign tongue. What language it could be was beyond Mr Straightly, who was well acquainted with most languages. The man was throwing his hands into the air as he spoke and letting them drop like leaves onto his lap but his eyes stayed closed and his face was near ecstatic.

Mr Straightly scratched at his few wisps of grey-ginger hair above his ears as his thoughts went back to an incident a few months before in London. Somehow, he had stumbled into a high class party where strange people were drinking and studying a newspaper, which was quite a rarity in itself these days; ever since the kids had bombed Fleet Street.

The paper included a tiny article exposing the existence of a hidden country that had been kept a closely guarded secret for years. Only a few old Buddhists had known about it, one of them being the exiled Dalai Lama himself. He was very old and wrinkled now. He claimed to be at least 150 years old but no one was sure.

One night, he revealed the existence of the secret country, telling its exact location. It was actually in Tibet itself but in a region previously thought to be too dangerous to inhabit. The Dalai Lama was a regular at the downtown orgies and had got a little too pissed and blurted the story to a whore. She immediately sold it to one of the few remaining reporters in the world for a ridiculous sum and soon it was just another talking point for those lucky enough to obtain the news.

Mr Straightly remembered the man who had shown and discussed the article with him. An oddball, he thought. All dressed up like a peacock with changeable hair colour and mandarin's shoes. Mr Bizarre was his name. He seemed to think the secret country was extremely important and said it was lucky that newspapers were so rare nowadays.

Mr Straightly snapped out of his memory and squinted through the Range Rover's window at the rain. It was pounding down heavily. He returned his attention to the plump man and wondered if he had just strayed from the road or actually been inside the secret country, for this was its location; it couldn't be far from here. Looking hard into the stranger's flushed face he was sure he recognised him, but dismissed the thought almost as quickly as it occurred. How could he possibly meet someone on the border between Tibet and Nepal and have met them before? He was leaning forward to have a closer look when the man suddenly burst out of his trance, turned his face towards the baffled Mr Straightly, opened his small eyes wide and said in a clear excited voice, 'I've seen it. I've seen it. I've seen it. I've seen it!'

I'VE SEENIT!
I'VE SEENIT!!!
SWISHHHHH
SWISHHHHH
SQUIRT!
SQUIRT!
SPLUDGE!
30473
©WILLY SMAX 1978

Chapter 3
The Amazing Trouser Escapade

'I say are you alright old chap, how about a shot of the old warm stuff? You look as though you need it.' Mr Straightly, doing his best to sound amiable, although he was somewhat in awe of the stranger who now suddenly looked older than before, offered the man a bottle of scotch.

'Ah, good on you sir. Trouser's the name. T.G. Trouser, must 'ave 'eard of me.' He guzzled the drink. 'Haven't met anyone yet who hasn't, if you see what I mean.' He have Mr Straightly a perplexed look as if hoping that man had not heard of him. Mr Straightly's head jerked back and a nervous twitch suddenly developed above his moustache.

'Gad! Trouser himself, what bally incompetence of me not to recognize you! My humble apologies sir. Um . . . Music Therapy forever, Trouser for king . . . By thunder!' Mr Straightly was bouncing up and down in the brown plastic seat, almost standing to attention sitting down.

'Oh you can skip all that old crap man, this is 2073, all those old slogans went out with space travel.'

'Ah, by George, of course, but one doesn't often have the honour of meeting the great T.G. Trouser himself and out here of all places. Oh yes, silly me, I'm forgetting myself. Straightly's the name, just Mr. Would you like a sandwich?'

'No thanks sport, for goodness sake don't sponk thyself on my behalf, I'm only humanoid after all . . . well almost.'

The great Trouser spoke with whatever accent suited him and managed to infuriate and baffle many who made his acquaintance, if acquaintance it could be called, for Trouser was a dark star in a strange sky. Right now he sounded remarkably Australian.

'I am indeed the great Trouser, sent down from on high to help the troubled world. The poor waif who never took yes or no for an answer, who pushed aside mediocrity and replaced it with mysticism. The untouchable, the alarming, the outrageous, the one and only T.G. Trouser and I thank you kind sir for your assistance.

He hit the bottle hard and then smiled genially at the awestruck Mr Straightly, extending a hand to shake in the unnatural silence. For the storm had stopped. The night was still and raindrops dribbled down the vehicle's window.

'It is a strange world, Mr Trouser sir. By Gad, what bally good fortune, I've always wanted to meet the man my good brother – God rest his soul – called the archbishop of inner space.'

'Your brother?'

'Ah yes, my brother. Great man in his own way.' Mr Straightly pursed his lips and thrust out his moustache, leaning on his elbow over the back of the driver's seat, twisting slightly to look into Trouser's face. 'Yes, good man, went and killed himself though. Used to work for you, though I don't suppose you'd remember him. Tall chappie, purple hair, used to be an M.T. attendant until he overloaded on a five-hour drum solo one day. Went out with a bang . . . the way he always wanted to go. Ah, good old Corset, where art thou a-wandering now?' Mr Straightly suddenly became melancholy and contemplative.

'Corset! Did you say Corset? Why I remember him well, always a dedicated worker. So you're his brother eh, too much. Used to idolize me. But there again that's not uncommon.'

Trouser looked out of the window and pointed out to Mr Straightly that the storm had stopped and they ought to be moving on.

'I've got a lot to do when I get back, oh yes indeedy, I gotta clean dem walkin' boots. Ever done any hiking, Straightly baby?'

'Oh, no old chap, read about it. Damn silly if you ask me. I say, whatever have you been up to out there; I do know a little about this hidden country business you know, word gets around.'

'Mr Bizarre been letting off steam again, has he? Well it can only be expected. Lucky I'm the only one left on earth with enough enterprise to go through with anything, isn't it? They'd all be trooping around here by now if they had the guts. Bastards.' Trouser stared straight ahead at the headlights dipping in and out of potholes in the track.

Mr Straightly looked baffled and carried on driving.

They reached the skyport in what used to be called India and awaited the arrival of a saucerette. It was a warm clear day and the two men sat in the bar drinking, looking out of the window onto the landing strip.

Trouser spoke: 'I'll tell you what, Mr Straightly, when we get back, I'll put you on Music Therapy for a year, free of charge. Any variation you may require; after all, you did save me from a gruelling walk. Never know, might never have made it here, and that's no way for the great Trouser to flash out. Corpsing in some grimy pothole. After all, there's a lot to be done yet, a lot to be done.'

'Sounds remarkably civil of you, Mr Trouser sir, by thunder I'm very honoured. Haven't had a good session in oh, let me see, must be at least four months, is it? Yes, a good four months. Could do with a few ah . . . kinks ironed out you know. Haven't been feeling myself lately.'

Trouser swivelled in his skyport chair and faced Mr Straightly. 'Who have you been feeling lately?'

Mr Straightly crossed his bare, white, hairy legs and straightened his khaki shorts, coughing slightly as he did. A customary nervous twitch just above his moustache had started. Trouser thought he looked like a cracked egg with a hedgerow growing across it. He had seen a book once called *Memories,* it was full of things like that. Things that were no more. Somehow the author had got them all mixed up though, hedgerows and eggs, chickens and Aldershot and District buses. 'Ahum yes . . . quite! quite! Oh look, here's our flight, Mr Trouser, what a beauty it is too. By Gad, I am glad I met you sir. Probably would have tried to get back by land otherwise. Never would have made it, of course.'

Mr Straightly jumped up from his seat nervously and cracked his naked kneecap on the bottom of the table. It was only a soft plastic table but it somehow dislodged something in his knee. He was left with a slight limp for the next three months. Nothing that Music Therapy couldn't take his mind off.

The saucerette was a ship large enough to carry 200 passengers, but being an early morning flight, Trouser and Straightly were the only people on board.

It was a wonderful silver disc glinting in the morning sunlight alone on the landing strip. There was no insignia on its silver surface to mar it in any way, just a black circle on the rearside indicating a door.

The two men, after delivering the Range Rover to the hold of the unmanned craft, made their way to the entertainments room. Mustering as much nerve and natural tact as he could, Straightly decided to grill the great Trouser, fearing he might never meet the man again in such a congenial mood. He began carefully, all the while twitching and scratching his drooping moustache.

'Tell me, Mr Trouser sir, if you don't mind my asking of course, what on earth have you been doing out there, and what's that funny smell . . . it's not ordinary incense, is it?'

Trouser pressed a button with an elegant finger and immediately six shutters slid back and six large windows appeared. The sunlight smashed into Mr Straightly's eyes until Trouser stepped in front of the sun. The room was still and the amusement machines bright but silent. Trouser's head, surrounded by the sun's golden red halo appeared to be burning in a great fire. His eyes looked dull as he at last answered the twitching, blinking Straightly.

'The funny smell, as you put it, Senor, is emitted from a remarkable substance called Pen-o-bip.' He seemed to be making a speech. 'An amazing compound taken internally which saturates the cells in gentle orgasm, the type of which I have never before experienced, in all my years of music therapy.'

'You mean, it actually soaks through your body and comes out smelling like that, preposterous! I mean – it's dumbfounding!'

'Yes, Mr Straightly, I might agree but for the fact that it is indeed true as your standing here!' Trouser suddenly scratched his clean shaven chin; he was wondering whether or not he'd said the last phrase right.

'Do you mean to tell me sir, this peno . . .o. . .'

'Pen-o-bip, Straightly.'

'Ah ha, Pen-o-bip is a substance from the um . . . hidden country?'

'Quite cleverly assumed, honeyrose.' Trouser spoke in a broad American accent. 'I mean like, Straightly baby, this is the big one, boy! Back in the old days they would'a called this Product. But for me it's a reawakening, yessir, Straightly old horse, a reawakening.' Trouser pressed another button which instantly shot milky fluid into double glazed windows and took the edge off the powerful sun. He was strutting around the room wagging his finger as he spoke, tapping the amusement tables with the gold ring on his left hand little finger.

'You'll see, brother, we's all been sat back on our asses, haw haw! Sat back on our collective asses athinking that the ole tried 'n trusted M.T. was the end, but no!' He slammed his hand on a machine sunk into the wall and out popped a card with the words 'Take an hour's augmented Sibelius Music Therapy and calm down' printed on it. 'Shan't!' shouted Trouser with glee; he was buffooning. 'Shan't! Shan't! Shan't!'

T.G. Trouser rushed up to the awestricken Straightly and stood with his face very close to him, his round bulbous nose almost touching Mr Straightly's and his green eyes gleaming. He whispered in English. 'I shan't, Mr Straightly: there's something in the air, we've all relied on M.T. for too bloody long. Continually look backwards as well as forwards my friend, for the past holds doors that were left only half open and the future may depend upon the opening of those doors.' He was still whispering at Straightly, whose eyes were wide with interest as well as astonishment. Trouser was speaking at his moustache and poor Straightly was dying to sneeze. The great Trouser continued.

'Inner space has had its day, it's a boring playground for mentally retarded wombats. We're being crippled by our own hideous introspection, man. I've created a monster. Outwards is the only way now boyo. Outwards.'

Mr Straightly sneezed and apologised all at once which made Trouser jump backwards. Just then the silent ship came to life and within seconds was airborne. It would take thirty minutes to get to London; meanwhile Trouser amused himself in the entertainments room. He was soon fed up wie video games and went on to the rat-splatter, a glass topped cabinet with a gun barrel pointing inside and trigger on the outside. Trouser gripped the gun and swivelled it around in eager anticipation. Suddenly a shutter opened at the far end of the table and a small vicious-looking rat ran out. It rushed around the inside until Trouser finally shot its head off. Unfortunately, springs and millions of wires protruded from the rat's torso instead of blood; you only got half a point for a synthetic rat. The scoreboard clicked up the score.

½ point – 1 shot

Still not bad, thought Trouser, only one shot.

Two more rats appeared from different holes and he took more time to consider before shooting. Phut!

'Wahey, got the bastard! Blew his testicles sideways.' Trouser laughed as the score flashed up and the other rat shot off back down the hole.

2½ points – 2 shots

The machine was splattered with blood and after three or four more successful hits it was getting difficult to judge where the target was.

'Tell you what, Straightly, best thing they ever did – put entertainments into these boring saucerettes, I mean. Something in the air, as I said. Something in the –'Phut! '–air! Got 'im, whadda killer-diller, must be nearly a top score!'

Trouser clapped his hands and did a little jig with his rotund body, shaking his golden curly head. He was apt to look like a mad puppet on occasions like these. Those early years of testing his music therapy devices had taken their toll on him. He'd been in some dark corners. Once, for a whole year he was stuck with the sound of all the black notes on a piano reverberating through his skull non-stop. It took him a lot of sound excursions to sort that one

WE'S ALL BEEN THINKING THAT MUSIC THERAPY WAS THE END! BUT OH NO!
TING!
KERONK!

TAKE AN HOURS AUGMENTED SIBELIUS MUSIC THERAPY AND CALM DOWN
SHAN'T!
I SHAN'T MR. STRAIGHTLY WE'VE RELIED ON MUSIC THERAPY FOR TOO LONG !!!!

INNER SPACE HAS HAD ITS DAY, WE'RE BEING CRIPPLED BY OUR OWN HIDEOUS INTROSPECTION
AH..AH..

OUTWARDS IS THE ONLY WAY NOW BOYO!
OUTWARDS!
AH..AH..AH..AH AH AH AH

CHOOO!!!

HUH, THAT RESPONSE TO A PHILOSOPHICAL CONCEPT CLEARLY EXPRESSES THE LAYMANS BASE ATTITUDE TO LIFE!

THINK I'LL GO ON THE RAT--SPLATTER
PEARLS BEFORE SWINE MUMBLE.....

WAHEY!
RAT-A-SPLAT SPLAT!!

out. The score lit up.

$10\frac{1}{2}$ points – 6 shots GENIUS MARKSMAN

'Of course, of course.'

The bottom dropped out and spray jets washed the blood and rat corpses away.

Later on when the two men were sitting drinking coffee and eating nutron pills, Trouser said he would keep in touch with Straightly, who bobbed and bowed in appreciation.

As they left the central London skyport Trouser handed him a tiny multi coloured capsule and said, 'Sorry about the sandwich refusal, take this and feel somebody else. Adios Monsieur.'

Mr Straightly frowned deeply, twitched his moustache and swallowed the capsule. For the next three days he wandered the sunny streets of London feeling a new man.

Chapter 4
Twiggott and the Large Squad

He sat in his bedroom on the floor with his back to the wall. He sported a brilliant turquoise mohican haircut to match the room, a skin-tight black T-shirt, a short maroon stenolin jacket with a huge pointed collar, amazing purple trousers, the bottoms of which were cut like a crown. And mock astronaut boots, one silver, one gold.

He was Twiggott.

Twiggott leaned his head against the yellow cushion fixed to the wall, sighed and blinked his blue eyes, absently dangling his arms between his open legs.

He'd just returned from Central Music Therapy after an exhausting two hour journey into his head. He usually visited the nastier places of his brain, plenty of hollow off-key piano overlayed with vibrosyzer, a conglomeration of sound only the more violent people could explore, and Twiggott was a rather nasty person. But only out of necessity as he would say; it was his destiny to be tough – he had his job to do.

The room was soaked in soft green light and an old Falling Parrot tape was blasting out. Twiggott lifted an arm idly and adjusted his haircut, making sure the bat-like collar was pointing up behind it, nice and stiff. He dropped his arm again and stuck his knees even wider apart. The afternoon's sessions had left him rather drained and even a little bored – he was waiting for the energy to pick up. When the boys came around he was sure to start feeling on top again.

Twiggott only just heard the buzzer through the rock'n'roll. He got up and strolled across the room. There was a small black microphone hanging over the bed which he lifted off its clip before falling onto the bed and stretching himself full length with legs astraddle, the huge grip soles on the astronaut boots jutting out like house bricks. He spoke through the mike; everything about him was relaxed and lazy. He literally enjoyed himself.

' 'Ello, 'oo is it then?'

' 'S me Twiggott, One'ser,' a voice answered from a tiny speaker in the microphone.

' 'Oo else?'

'Jus' me 'n Two'ser'.

'You and Two'ser eh, awright, up comes ya.'

Twiggott replaced the microphone, and dropped his head on the green pillows. His haircut tilted forward just level with his eyes. He stared at the ceiling.

There was a gentle knock on the door. Twiggott said, 'Enter,' and a small square face peered around the half-open door. His eyebrows were raised as if asking Twiggott if it was alright to come in and his jet black hair stood up on end. He looked like he'd just had a nasty shock.

'Come,' said Twiggott.

The door opened wider and One'ser stepped in, followed closely by Two'ser.

'How does it move boys,' said Twiggott.

'Well y'know, 's alright; goin' out are we?'

One'ser sat on the side of the bed with his right foot resting across his left knee. He picked the bottom of his boot which was like Twiggott's, only smaller and yellow. Two'ser leaned back on the green door and just stared into the floor, his lips creased into a smirk.

'I should think we can afford a stroll, boys, just a little stroll townwise ta see where the ball rolls like, just a loud crunch through da streets of London town to shake the ole molecules lifewise, eh lads?' Twiggott was already beginning to feel on top again.

'Yeah . . . good ole Twigg! When we off?'

Two'ser came to life and stood up straight, then he started flexing his arms about and bending at the knees in a parody of his excitement.

Both boys wore tight stenolin jackets, bright yellow with a black stripe up the back and yellow floppy cossack trousers tight at the bottoms and tucked inside their boots. They called them banana suits.

The tape finished playing and Twiggott slid off the bed and walked over to a cabinet with a mirror jutting from its top. He looked in the mirror and smiled at the boys, opening a drawer in the cabinet as he did so. Inside the drawer were hundereds of Music Therapy 'Holiday Pods' in round perspex containers, each type indentifiable by the tiny coloured dots imprinted on them. He took out six of the small black pods, quickly examining the colour codes. Three he placed in his pocket, one he put in his right ear, the other two he gave to the boys who in turn stuck them in their ears.

Twiggot opened the door and gestured to the boys to walk through, clicking his vast heels together and looking slick and animated. Two'ser shuffled his feet with a grin and stepped out, closely followed by the swaggering One'ser. The Twiggott spun around and slipped a pencil-thin electric walking cane off a hook on the wall, smacked it across his right shoulder and sleeked out of the room slamming the door behind him.

The street was an explosion of colours, lights and laughter; bodies of every shape and size shuffled along the plastic pavement which changed colour with every footfall. Between the pavements the bubble chairs glided along on rollers mostly full with bright people.

Twiggott stepped out, swinging his thin cane and occasionally moving his green haircut forward. He looked a star. The lights from the stores seemed to pick him out deliberately, he was a bright beacon of radiant colour in the electric night air.

One'ser and Two'ser were close on his heels trying to look as good but not quite succeeding. They knew he was a born leader. They threw haughty glances at the shuffling people they passed – sometimes One'ser would chase off small children who accidentally bumped into them. They were well known in the city as protectors of the cause, Music Therapy. How much they did exactly was uncertain, but they did seem to have an air of authority about them. They rarely hit innocent people but when they did it was never challenged; boys will be boys, and these boys were very special. They were employed by one T.G. Trouser as bodyguards. Twiggott was a close associate of the great Trouser and had been for some years. They'd helped each other through dark times.

Crossing a bridge over the road the three lads headed for Piccadilly Circus which was a pleasure dome of many facets. Indeed its surface seemed to reflect what happened inside. It looked like a massive fly's eye in a riot of ever-changing colours. To all who entered, it was like the centre of the universe where earthly delights mixed in unison with high spirituality. You could forget yourself in the dome, and people needed to forget themselves, especially these days. There was little else to do.

As they approached the flashing dome, three figures swung through a revolving door in the front of a large department store and headed in Twiggott's direction. They were dressed in immaculate white suits with red plastic T-shirts and black mock astronaut boots. They had spikey green hair jutting out around their ears and black conical hats. Twiggott greeted each with his name.

'Three'ser, Four'ser, Fiv'ser. Awright boy'sers, 'ow's yer collective 'ead? Pop this.'

With a relaxed smile, he handed each one a black Holiday Pod, and then carried on sauntering towards the pleasure dome where loud music rocked through the colour.

One'ser, Two'ser, Three'ser, Four'ser and Five'ser folowed closely. They were the Large Squad.

Twiggott and the Large Squad.

Through humo-plastic corridors leading to fleshy rooms they strolled, tasting a different experience in each room, in each facet of the dome. There were temples full of bald meditating monks, grape rooms whose walls ran with wine, simulated jungles thick with giant hemp-plants and Tarzan imitators. Black rooms for death. White rooms for bliss. Shifting-perspective-floors-walls-and-ceilings rooms, for confusion. Little rooms piled high with cushions where beautiful women beckoned, stroking Persian cats. There was a muscle gallery, the ultimate in butch experience; the gentle river, a subtle stream of radiating light.

All this and more in the pleasure dome, a post-Trouser creation of great value. Twiggott and the Large Squad stayed for a few bloated hours sampling many delights before bathing in the bone bath and slipping out into the buzzing night.

'Well, Boy'sers, 'ow about soya an' scotch and then I think a little visit. You do know of whom I'm a-ramblin' of, Boy'sers? Go an' visit some old friends shall we? Pay a little social call jus'ta see what those two wombats is up to, eh?'

'Eeeeee yeah Twig! Le's go and do 'em,' answered Four'ser.

'Jerry Can and Toni the Cortina, is I right, Twiggott?' said One'ser.

'You is One'ser, you is. But let's not be too . . . 'asty.' Twiggot slapped

BOM DIDDY BOM!
SCREAM!!!
PLUG IN, AND WE'LL GO DOWN 'THE DOME!
TA!
GOODY!
GOODY!
GOODY!
GROAN!

ASTRO HOTEL
ASTRO HOTEL
FLICK!
POP!

LOVE
THE ARCADE OF ANGER
THE HOUSE OF JOY
NAME YOUR

himself hard across the shoulder with his walking cane and stood with his slim legs astraddle, the boy'sers gathering around in the neon night air outside the back of the pleasure dome.

'After all, they've been quietish jus' lately, those two hellish wombats. Probably scrapping for the next nutron pill, poor pealies ahhhhh . . .'

Twiggot laughed loud and fresh in the night and swaggered along over the road bridge of thin stylish silver metal with the Large Squad clicking their boots along behind him.

The bubble chairs slipped along underneath them as they crossed but many of them were empty now; it was early morning.

Chapter 5
Jerry Can and Toni the Cortina

'Fer panks sake man, wh . . . what the hell are we gonna do if we get attacked now? I mean Christ man, tho . . . those large bastards and that panking Twiggott fella again, I . . . I'm gonna get a big stick I tell ya!'

Jerry Can was Irish and emaciated. He had brown hair, and a kiss curl often swung into his face only to be pushed back again. His pale sunken green eyes looked nervously about him as he spoke over a curly nose to his partner, Toni the Cortina.

'Now take it easy J.C. We've been quiet lately, haven't we? There's been no raids of any description. There's been no protests or arm twisting in any quarter. Even when the intrepid – or should I say tepid – Trouser, pissed off on his own in such a suspicious manner last month. I mean, we both know about Javaal, the secret country, don't we? We know what that crook's up to. Daft as a pill that Trouser. I'll slice him up one sweet day, J.C. then me and you can get back together like the old days. Artificial organs at exorbitant prices; one free lung with every two transplanted! Ah back to those simple days of dedication; transplants. That's what the world needs again. Transplants.'

Toni the Cortina seemed melancholy and absorbed in his dream. He couldn't give up what he'd strived for all his life. A man must have a purpose. Just because the trends go one way doesn't necessarily mean it's the right way. Besides, Trouser was such a clown underneath it all. A tubby old fool. He wanted slicing. Toni the Cortina was slim and tall and agile. He was also very tough and had done dealings with Twiggott before now.

The strange thing was, they'd been in the same embryo chamber together and had been good friends in their early life. Toni the Cortina's father had thought Twiggott to be such a nice playmate for his little orange-haired son. Toni the Cortina's father was a great pioneer of artificial organs. A master transplant surgeon.

He'd passed his knowledge on to his son who in turn was considered a near genius. Toni the Cortina, however, was to make the acquaintance of Jerry Can, a no-good brain surgeon from New Belfast. Jerry Can introduced him to the art of relaxation and Mad-Rubber squeezing and an enjoyable disintegration soon followed. They'd had their good times though, these boys. But it was so hard to live like a king without the backing of a vast business. They were underground now. Them and their henchies, testingly called the Round Lads, a name Twiggott opposed violently. He had attacked them with great vigour and vehemence the day they were formed.

'Look Toni, you know if that Twiggott fella . . . kindaway, grooves round here now, we're clobbered! Look man . . . the . . . the Round Lads might not be back fer hours, man. You should never of told them not to bother comin' back until they'd got some provisions. I mean tha's daft man. Are ya . . . kindaway, losing yer head?'

'Oh, you're just a worrier, J.C. Roll out some more Mad-Rubber and take it easy. If they were going to come here tonight I'd just intercom the Lads and they'd be back in a flash, no rankle.'

Jerry Can shrugged and got up. He walked over to the large french windows and looked out. In the darkness he could see most of the lawn and the fountains with their gargoyles spewing forth water. He could just make out the main gate but didn't feel any relief at the thought of the 50,000 volts it carried.

With hands in mock denim pockets he loped across the big white and yellow room to a series of video screens embedded in the wall. One covered the road just outside the main gate, another two swivelled around the garden and two more surveyed the back of the house. Their tiny cameras were well hidden.

Jerry Can pulled some pieces of fresh emerald-coloured Mad-Rubber out of its wrapper, turning his head from side to side like a child playing with a toy. There was a block of the stuff the size of his fist on the polished table. Squeezing the two small portions together he fell back into an armchair, a happy smile spreading over his face as he kneaded out the Mad-Rubber's vital stimulant in his right hand.

Toni stretched out on the chaise-longue and stared absently through the windows, focusing on the rather corny fountains. He was wondering if Westminster Abbey was missing its gargoyles. He scratched his leg, straightened his orange tunic which matched his crispy hair, and yawned as he spoke.

'Ah . . . well, I don't suppose they'll be too long now. Just a few provisions, that's all.'

'Yeah well, okay man, but we'll not have any cartoons on until they do, tha's for sure, I'm keeping my panking ears open, I tell ya.'

Jerry Can sidled over the room to Toni and plonked himself beside him, passing the lump of emerald Mad-Rubber.

'I wanna know what that Trouser fella's up to, tha's what I wanna know, man. I reckon we should clobber that daft bastard quick. I mean, for Chrissakes Toni, the whole thing 'ud fall ta pieces, you know. I s'pose you know that, do yer? Without him I reckon half the world would collapse, you should see 'em, man, they idolise the bastard. What it is he's got I don't know, I'm sure. I think he's a right wombat. Daft as a trout. Why d'yer 'member that time I was posing as a psychoanalyst in Music Therapy Centre, hey remember that? When I caught him with a spanner down his pants havin' an erotic experience over one of those old fashioned workshop manuals. A picture of a back axle or somethin', sure he was. I ask yer, what kind of a fella does that sort of thing? I mean, an' when I tell's people there, they say I'm losing my panking . . . kindaway . . . losin' my bearin's take a course they tell me, get down on a couch an' . . . an' iron yer cells out with some gentle sound. Pank man. Gnatpiss for the masses! I know how to keep my head, even in these times, I don't need Music Therapy, Christ!'

Jerry Can looked exasperated, his liquid Irish eyes wide and pale, he squeezed the Mad-Rubber again. Toni the Cortina's eyes had closed. He had a vision of Trouser in his mind. Square and fumbling, golden hair, vacant eyes. A buffoon with magic, a clever bastard too, in his own way.

The moon was still and no sound came from the garden save for the tinkling fountains. J.C. leaned his head back and looked at the white and yellow checked ceiling for a while before closing his eyes. Neither could be bothered to switch the mellow lamp on in the corner and turn the main light off; it was excessively bright in the room. J.C. dreamed the electric dream between wishing it wasn't all so hard. He forgot about Twiggott for a moment and anything connected with T.G. Trouser. He even forgot they were unprotected while the video screens in the corner blacked out, one by one.

Silence.

In a mindscape of ginger cats, chasing different coloured dogs through pretty streets, J.C. heard a tap, tap, sound. He thought it was in his head at first but again he heard it, louder this time. He realized with a shock it was coming from the french windows. Toni the Cortina and Jerry Can opened their eyes almost together and there, grinning through the windows in the silence, pressed against the glass, with the black night behind them and the bright light of the room picking them out like flies, were Twiggott and the Large Squad.

There were eight big panes of glass; On Twiggot's right Three'ser, Four'ser and Five'ser were pressed against the window bearing sardonic grins and looking identical, a triple image of a nasty clown.

One'ser and Two'ser were on Twiggot's left in their banana suits. One'ser was wiggling his fingers in a mock wave, doing a drum roll on the glass with the tips of his fingers. Two'sers black hair stuck skywards, and his eyes were wide open in a parody of poor J.C. and Toni the Cortina's obvious shock.

Twiggott stood still in the centre with his legs astraddle, arms folded and head tilted to the side with a slight crease in his lip, his vast mock astronaut boots bright and clear through the window. He regarded the startled pair with a cold eye before breaking out in a large grin as he raised his hand, adjusted his hair cut, and brought his hand down through the window hard and fast.

J.C. and Toni the Cortina scrambled to their feet in panic and made for the back of the room where a yellow and white chequered door stood slightly ajar. They collided with each other in the attempt to escape and tumbled through the door into a big hall with a black and white chequered floor. They were sprawled like idiots on the floor screaming but managed to get up and make for the back of the hall as Twiggott and the Large Squad strolled through the broken window. Twiggott sauntered ahead and signalled to one of the lads to pick up the Mad-Rubber on the table.

One'ser gleamed and picked it up, biting off a chunk and squeezing it in his hand.

Five'ser knew what to do. He rushed back outside and took the sticky tape off the camera lens. He would soon stroll back and watch the videos for signs of the Round Lads.

J.C. and Toni the Cortina had rushed to the back of the hall and pulled two long slim silver swords from the green wall. The hall had once been a

JERK!
THPLURT!
PAT-A-PAT-A-PAT-A-PAT-A-TAP-TAP-TAP!
EH?!
PORTCULLIS
WILLY SMAX © COPYRIGHT 1979

gymnasium but there was no need for that sort of thing now. They stood with their backs to the wall –they knew they should have used the other door and maybe even have escaped out of the back. But they were too erased and panic-stricken to sort it out.

Toni the Cortina swished the sword and moved a few paces away from the wall. J.C. was open-eyed and sweaty, pressed hard against the wall wondering how to use a sword. He was more worried about whether it would anger Twiggott any more than was necesary. Damn Toni the Cortina! Where were the Round Lads?

'Well, well, well! What kind of wombats do we 'ave 'ere then? We comes round. A little social visit an' what 'appens?'

Twiggott looked around him at the Large Squad. 'I tell ya what 'APPENS, BOY'SERS. They pick bloody swords up. That's all; SWORDS!' he shouted.

'Tch, tch. Ya can't even 'ave a little commune wiv yer old playmates wivout dem aturnin' on ya.'

He was a great actor.

One'ser was leaning against the wall, one yellow-clad leg hooked over the other, looking up occasionally between squeezes of Mad-Rubber at Twiggott performing. He winked and nodded and frowned in mock scorn, overplaying his agreement.

J.C. dropped his sword in shock, it echoed in the hall. 'N . . . Now look here, Twiggott. We've bin quiet, man. We . . . We've caused no . . . ah . . . kindaway . . . caused no trouble.'

Twiggott pretended not to listen and stared at Toni the Cortina, who started swishing the pliable sword about. He was fond of watching very old films and had a large collection of them. He threw himself into an Errol Flynn fantasy; it was the only way he could work up the courage to face this situation.

'Well, you better pick dat sword up, Jerry Can. There was another silly bastard with the same initials as you once an' they crucified 'im. TAKE 'EM!' Twiggott shouted the order and the Large Squad splayed out across the room, surrounding the two and closing in.

Twiggott, still in the centre, took off his haircut and pulled out of it a small pink plastic phial with a black button on top, all the while staring at Toni the Cortina who was trying to look swashbuckling.

'Silly kiddos! I'll crack yer 'eads eggish, I will. Trouser opposition is black-looked upon. You need a dental job, tha's what!'

J.C. had picked up his sword and was half-heartedly threatening Two'ser with it.

Two'ser kneeled down calmly and undid his boots. He took them off and waved them from side to side like big boxing gloves. Meanwhile, the rest of the Large Squad closed in with him around poor Jerry Can whose Irish eyes were crying.

Toni the Cortina suddenly charged at Twiggott who was almost caught out. He hadn't expected such pluck, but he ducked the blow from the silver sword and danced backwards, squirting a muddy black fluid from the pink phial. The fluid was aimed true and it shot all over Toni the Cortina's face. It

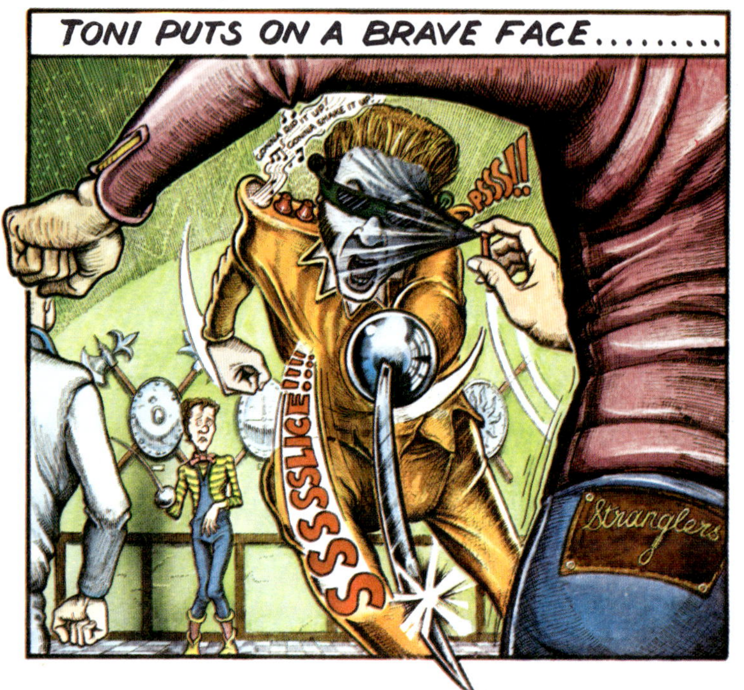

hardened immediately and gripped his skin like a huge scab. He could see nothing after that. It would take an hour before the substance crystallized and flaked off.

He had to drop the sword after a while, and pointlessly tore at the scab which covered his eyes and part of his forehead and which gripped the bridge of his nose hideously. He realized he was quite lucky in a way; if the fluid had hit his eyeballs directly, it would have dried and cracked them – eggish.

'I tell ya what Wombie, you pretend not ta see me, an' I'll kick ya in the 'ead.'

Which is just what Twiggott did. Toni the Cortina fell to the ground with blood shooting out of his ear. He fell with his head on a white chequer which pleased Twiggott no end.

'Aha . . . checkmate! ARTIFICIAL ORGANS? Well, you're gonna need a new ear for a start!'

He kicked again and almost cracked Toni the Cortina's left hip. Twiggott would have carried on if it wasn't for the blood on his boot. He scowled angrily and clicked off towards the door to clean it. It was the gold one; he didn't like that sort of thing.

In the far corner, however, J.C. was being unusually defensive. Swishing his sword about angrily, he had already taken a chunk out of Two'sers boot. Two'ser smiled idiotically, finally throwing about deftly, to knock the sword from J.C.'s hand.

They soon laid Jerry Can out on the floor and stood on his hands and legs whilst Four'ser practiced the latest dance craze on his stomach. Jerry Can's moaning filled the hall.

When Twiggott was in the lounge and wiping his bloody boot with a white cushion, he realized with a shock that all the Large Squad were in the hall enjoying Jerry Can. Twiggott rushed over to the video screens just in time to see four figures approaching the main gate; two were carrying large plastic sacks, no doubt filled with spoils. He could just make out in the dark that they were dressed rather drably. All in olive kharki. Twiggott felt suddenly very proud of the Large Squad.

Twiggott bounded back into the hall where Toni the Cortina was sprawled unconscious. The Large Squad were taking it in turns to throw Two'sers yellow boots at poor Jerry Can, cringing against the wall.

'Sorry ta crack the party breakwise, boy'sers; we've got visitors.'

They all stopped and looked around. Five'ser was just about to fling a left boot and dropped it with a start, realizing he'd forgotten to stay with the videos. He hated missing out on the action.

'S . . . Sorry Twigg. I forgot, sorry.'

'Don't get soppish, kiddo, there's no need to turn brown on my behalf; get yer boots on, Two'ser quick! These *Round Lads* are a bloody irkish lot. I don't wanna get any more blood on me boots – let's splinter.'

They left their victims in the chequered hall. Toni the Cortina had come to, but still feigned unconsciousness – just in case. Jerry Can was curled up in the corner rubbing his hand; it felt broken.

There was a bell ringing in the lounge as Twiggott and the Large Squad lumbered through; the Round Lads were waiting for the gates to open.

Twiggott raised his hair cut at the Round Lads and shouted abuse before slinking off in the darkness to the back of the grounds where they helped each other over the high brick wall.

Four'ser put his boot through the video screens before they left, just for the hell of it. It had been a good night. On the way back, One'ser collapsed in a heap in the dark road with an incredible stomach ache. He couldn't stop laughing. He'd accidentally eaten some of the Mad-Rubber and had the feeling he was too heavy to walk now; he was laughing into the drain and talking to imaginary people. 'C'mon outa there, you, I know there's someone down there! Hey, Twigg, look at this, there's someone down the drain! Loads of green Wombies down there, look at 'em!'

They carried him home laughing.

Chapter 6
Bruce

When Notting Hill Gate had been demolished in 1986, the Authorities – what was left of them – had breathed a sigh of relief. The place was a threat to all decent god-fearing folk and a nest of revolutionaries of all descriptions. Militant blacks, all-in mud wrestlers, prostitute transvestites, Devil worshippers, rogue lion tamers, Trouserites (Trouser at that time was still considered to be a threat), and many more sinister phenomena.

It was a great stroke of idiocy pulled by a Water Board technician in the Spring of 1984 to add even more chemicals to the separate water supply of the workers. The man was Wahin Tabloid McKnicker, a Chinese Scot born in India, whose name was destined to go down in history, as he'd always envisaged.

The new formula he'd been working on was designed, like many others of its kind, to nullify the increasingly unpredictable new mental evolution, now occurring uncontrolled within the psyche of the human race. Like many other new additives it was hurriedly administered in the vague hope of dampening the inflamed awareness and attention span of the masses. And in the frenzy to return to the straight-forward days of leaders and followers, conclusive tests were ignored as Wahin's potent brew was shot, unceremoniously, into the reservoirs, seas and waterways of the world. The chemical triggered the final mental detonation and mass upheaval followed, leaving everyone floundering in the Year of the Silent Bang, as it was later to be known. It was the beginning of a new era. The reign of the Trouser. Saviour, peacemaker, squanderer, buffoon, T.G. Trouser.

Notting Hill was now a cone-shaped complex of living quarters designed by a brilliant man who had a bee fixation. On the ground floor, in Apartment L.O.D., lived Mr Straightly.

He lived very simply in his little circular room, playing with toy soldiers most of the time and reading his father's books on survival in the jungle. On the wall was a great moose's head with big sad eyes that seemed to smile and regard Mr Straightly with humour. He would often look up and say things to it like, 'Gad, my father must have had nerves of steel to pot a big fellow like you, old chap.' Or sometimes he would threaten it and throw bits of rolled-up paper, diving behind his antique sofa to safety. He didn't know that these animals were, when they still existed, vegetarians. He thought they were man eaters and extremely dangerous. It had been his ambition, however, to shoot a tiger, but now they were extinct and his dream was quashed. He honestly didn't know what to live for.

Mr Straightly was eating soya bread and vegipills when a sound came from the mail chute, which meant something was coming in. There was light plop as a blue envelope slipped from the silver chute, and fell lightly into the wicker basket. His eyes opened with a start and he spilt his tea down his bare leg, cursing out loud as the hot brown liquid scorched the gingerish hairs: 'Bally sod it! Oh damn it all.' He got up hastily and wiped his leg with a tea cloth; he still wore the khaki shorts which came down to just two inches above the knee. He looked at the envelope sitting in the basket cautiously as if it might be explosive, lifting his white hunter's hat from his head to scratch a bright shiny bald pate, while a frown creased his forehead.

He was about to pick it up when he decided to comb what was left of his hair first. There were a few wisps and bristles at the back of his head and around his ears. Looking in the mirror at his permanently baffled face, he wondered who the letter could be from, although he was almost certain anyway. It would be a letter from his old Auntie Paperclip, his only living relative, and a silly old fool at that. He hated the letters he got from her but read them over and over again, despite his loathing. She was always asking for things he couldn't give her, and enquiring after his mental health. He picked up the letter and noticed for the first time that the address had been typed, not written.

It was from someone else. Then Mr Straightly ripped it open hurriedly, and inside he found a tight scroll of polypaper which he stretched out and examined. The white words, impregnated on the transparent polypaper, read like this:

TO WHOM IT MAY CONCERN (MR STRAIGHTLY)
YOU ARE CORDIALLY HEREBY WHEREWITH, INVITED TO THE OCCASION OF THE DECADE. AN AMALGAMATION OF TENTACLE IMPORTANCE BEJEWELLED BY SOME (IF NOT ALL) OF THE MOST PERFORCE CARICATURES IN THE HISTORY OF THE WORLD (MUSIC THERAPY 1987) (P.O.N.K.) WITH WHICH YOU SHALL ATTEND, ARMED WITH TEETH, AND LIKE IT – OR ELSE.
A BALL PARTY FOR CABBAGES WILL BE THROWN AT MY RESIDENCE 8 P.M. FRIDAY THE 12TH JUNE. 2073.
AT THE INFAMOUS TROUSER HOUSE, TINT STREET.
PLEASE DO NOT MOUTH OFF AND DO NOT INFORM ANY CRASHERS OF THE NO-GOOD VARIETY NOR ODDBODS OF ANY DEROGATORY NATURE, ANTI-TROUSER OR SIMILAR.
YOURS WITH A WINK,
T.G. TROUSER
(MUSIC THERAPY LTD.)
P.S. ADIOS TILL THEN. LOOK EXQUISITE AND BRING A FRIEND.

'By thunder! Mr Trouser wants me – to attend an occasion?' Mr Straightly gasped as he picked the words out. This was the most exciting thing that had ever happened to him; he was astounded. Eyes all a-sparkle, he danced a little jig, waving the letter around with his thin white arm.

'A party, a party. I'm going to a party!' He sang loud and joyful, and started flinging toy soldiers at the uncomprehending moose's head until he was quite tired. Then he remembered what it said at the bottom of the letter. He looked at it again.

'AND BRING A FRIEND.'

A wave of frustration passed through him for a moment when he read this. He knew he'd look silly if he didn't take someone with him. Why has there always got to be a complication? 'Bally tomrot!' he sanpped. He didn't really have any friends; apart from Auntie Paperclip, whom he hated, he was quite alone. Mr Straightly scratched his red scalp again and squeezed his lips tightly together.

He sighed. 'Oh dear . . . still, mustn't let a little thing like that mar the proceedings, must we? No, certainly not. Keep the old school walking! I'll go out and find a bally friend. That's what. Can't keep me down.' He jumped up and put a bright yellow tie on, over an orange striped shirt, beaming in his mirror. 'The Great Trouser has called me, can't miss out on this chance of a lifetime.'

He pulled on a sports coat and purple trousers, then he put his best orangy-brown plastic brogues on, and a wonderful Panama hat he'd picked up in a church jumble sale before the religious organizations had finally owned up and collapsed under force.

The dashing Mr Straightly hopped on a bubble chair bound for Electic City, a giant fun-house three miles square, just south of the river. He smiled brightly at everyone in sight and twirled his moustach as the bubble chair flashed along in the sunlight.

When Mr Straightly reached Electric City, he realized he had no idea how to go about actually making a friend. Should he walk through the gardens and bump into someone and start talking to them? Should he go to one of the hundreds of happy discotheques and learn to dance? No, they'd only laugh at him. Perhaps he was looking for a really sincere friend and not just someone to accompany him to the Great Trouser's party. Someone he could share his elation with, perhaps.

'AND BRING A FRIEND.'

The words echoed in his mind.

It seemed to Mr Straightly that some things never changed, whatever diversions we sourrounded ourselves with, we were still at the mercy of our circumstances. He realized he must snap out of this philosophical train of thought; to make a friend, one had to bubble outside but hold a blank inside. One had to be shallow and untroubled by negative thought, for surely, philosophy of any kind was negative thought when it came down to making friends. Maybe, he thought, he would meet a philosophical person. Someone he could relate to, but then, they would probably be cleverer than him and leave him groping for words; it wouldn't be the first time that had happened.

No, he would play this by ear – there was sure to be a good chance, if the weather holds.

There were so many people walking through the various groves, grottos and mazes of Electric City that Mr Straightly felt immediately confident of something nice happening. He straightend the yellow tie, unbuttoned his sports coat, and immersed himself in the gay, flowing mass. The people were as one being in Electric City. They rolled and laughed and danced in controlled confusion. There were roundabouts and roller coasters, fat ladies and good fairies, fortune tellers, huge plastic elephants that lit up in different colours, tiny tube-like alleyways that looked as though only one person could go through at a time but, in fact, stretched like rubber when a crowd walked into them. All the while, balloons fell from the sky and different-coloured ribbons were blown from holes in the walls, while everything changd tone and illumination repeatedly.

Mr Straightly felt decidedly euphoric at once and his cheeks glowed with health and vigour. Every now and then he would do a little dance and people around him would burst into laughter and dissipate almost immediately. No one minded, Electric City was a place to perform, a place of release.

Mr Straightly felt he'd been twirling round and round for hours when he popped through a tiny tube alleyway and out into a sunlit park. He was confronted by a blue lake and green grass with flower beds of all shapes and shades, and huge birds with wonderful fan-like feathers, spreading and flexing. The lake seemed to stretch right into the horizon, but Mr Straightly believed this to be some kind of illusion.

He certainly felt very strange now: Electric City had that effect on people. Every time you went there it was completely different. He seemed to be remarkably relaxed and rubbery and slightly weak at the knees, especially the left one, he still had a slight limp from that fateful meeting with T.G. Trouser.

The atmosphere in the park was perfectly still and Mr Straightly looked around. Behind him, and arching away to his left, was a vast flesh-like wall with tube alleyway holes dotted into the distance, probably encircling the park. There were people popping out of the holes every now and again and rushing down to the lake happily. He could barely evade the feeling of agoraphobia. Was this real? He wasn't sure that it mattered anyway, and everyone else seemed quite calm, so he stepped onto the gravel path that ran the perimeter of the blue lake.

He noticed a dark, elegant figure approaching him, a man in a heavy blue coat and homburg, tapping a red can. Mr Straightly remembered the original intention of his visit and decided to try and make this man his friend.

As the figure came closer, Mr Straightly felt sweat prickling his palms and his moustache started its twitching again. He was determined to have a go, so he applied some light conversation.

'Ah . . . Hul . . . Hullo . . . ah . . . good day to you, sir.' He smiled nervously. The man, however, didn't make any sign.

'Such a wonderful park this, isn't it, wouldn't you say? Ah . . . such bally good weather for the time of year too. Topping, what?'

Mr Straightly was at his most amiable, and now the man had noticed him after what seemed an eternity. He took off his homburg and revealed a very startling head of rainbow-coloured hair which cascaded gently onto his shoulders.

'Good day to you, sir. I trust you're enjoying yourself?'

Mr Straightly was confused by this comment; he wasn't sure how he should answer it. The man's hair held his attention – it didn't fit with his clothes. Mr Straightly found himself reminded of his childhood for some reason. He remembered how sick he was one day after he'd eaten curry and peppermint creams mixed together. That was long before nutron pills.

'Ah . . . yes, of course; Straightly's the name, just Mr.'

'Glad to make your acquaintance, Mr Straightly.' The man spoke in a gruff, businesslike voice and extended a hand. When they shook hands, it sounded very loud in the still, warm air. A large bird squawked on the lake, the sound seemed to reverberate. 'Mr Curpep at your service, businessman, ridiculous. Come here often, do you? What's your line?'

'Oh yes, Mr Curpep; you did say Curpep? Me? Oh this and that, you know, this and that. A bit of this . . . and a bit of that.'

Mr Straightly was a little at a loss for words really. Conversation had never been his strong point, but this man, although somewhat disturbing, might make a good friend – to take to the Great Trouser's party at any rate.

They soon found themselves walking along the path around the lake. Mr Straightly was getting uncomfortably warm so he took his sports coat off. The other man seemed untroubled; a calm, self-confident smile on his face all the while. He tapped his red cane and pointed out to some large swans peacefully dipping around in the calm crystal water.

'Wonderful creatures, don't you think so, Mr Straightly? Sublime and serene, always remind me of my poor departed mother, deep in heaven.'

'Yes, aren't they! Pity we haven't got anything to feed them with. Gad, it's so peaceful here, I don't feel myself at all today, it's silly . . .'

'Don't you?' said the man. 'Hm, well you should try it sometimes, it's not all bad, you know.' He glanced almost expectantly at Mr Straightly, who was looking around uncomprehendingly, scratching his red, bald head, his Panama hat limp in his hand.

'Oh, of course, nearly forgot. Here we are.' Mr Curpep pulled a brown paper bag from his pocket. 'Soya bread,' he gestured to Mr Straightly. 'For the swans.'

'By thunder, how marvellous!' He bounced up and down, bending his knees. 'Let's sit down and feed the little blighters, eh?'

They sat on the grassy bank, with the sunlight flooding everything. Mr Curpep still kept his thick coat on; his hat he laid down between himself and Mr Straightly. In the distance a couple laughed and vanished into a dark green patch of luxuriant undergrowth.

Ripping chunks from the slabs of deep brown soya bread and flinging them to the swans made Mr Straightly feel so happy and childlike, he couldn't help but laugh. It was so infectious that Mr Curpep soon found himself joining in, shaking his rainbow hair and slapping his knees in delight as the great white swans stretched their necks and gulped down the bread.

They were almost in hysterics, rocking back and forth on the grassy bank. Mr Straightly had turned bright red from head to toe. He was hardly aware of what he was doing as he, by mistake, picked up Mr Curpep's brown homburg and started to rip it to pieces.

Before long, he'd fed all of it to the swans who seemd to enjoy it as much as the bread.

They continued laughing madly until Mr Curpep reached across for his hat.

'Oh, oh, my goodness, Mr Straightly. I . . . I really must get going. I've got a board meeting this afternoon. I really must control this laughter by the time

. . . Where's my hat?'

'Your what? Your hat? By Gad, it's just down here, sir.' Mr Straightly put his head in his hands and carried on tittering but Mr Curpep was suddenly looking very anxious.

'For goodness sake, man, snap out of it! Where's my damn homburg? It was down here a minute ago; next to the bread. Where the hell's it gone?'

It was then that Mr Curpep looked at the swans, who were fighting over a piece of dark material just a few yards from the bank.

Mr Straightly's eyes followed soon after, and he felt a cold shock pass through him. His moustache twitched along with a little vein just under his right eye, and his hands came up to his mouth suddenly. He had turned quite pale.

Mr Curpep spoke with rage creeping into his voice. 'MY HAT! My Hat! You've ripped my prize possession to pieces! My . . . my homburg, handed down by my grandfather to my mother, who used to wear it too! Why, it was almost an antique. Is nothing safe these days?! Can't a fellow put his panking hat down without some bloody fool coming along, ripping it to pieces, and feeding it to the bloody swans? Eh? Well, answer me!'

He was getting unreasonable now, and poor Mr Straightly didn't know what to do with himself.

'Oh goodness, how bally silly of me. I just don't know what came over me. I just thought it was the bread . . . I . . . I didn't look.'

'You didn't WHAT!'

'I . . . I, oh, damn bally! Look, Mr Curpep, I'll buy you another one . . . two even . . . anything. I didn't feed your hat to the swans on purpose, honestly.'

Mr Curpep's broad, dark face looked hot and heavy, He had his big right hand resting on his knee and to Mr Straightly he suddenly looked a little dangerous. He spoke through his teeth. 'You, Sir, are a cad. A scallywag of the worst variety. And most probably a practicing anti-Trouser!'

'No, me? I have the greatest respect. . .' But before Mr Straightly could finish, Mr Curpep jumped to his feet, stamped up and down for a bit, and then crouched down quickly, thrusting his face close to Mr Straightly. He looked him the eye, his rainbow hair hanging in lank strands around his face.

He whispered nastily, 'You, Sir, have not heard the last of this.'

With that he swiftly poked his finger in Mr Straightly's left eye. Then he jumped up, brushed his coat down and strode off down the gravel path without once looking back.

Mr Straightly could only look on incredulously, with his eyes watering profusely.

He closed his eyes sadly, trying to determine just what had happened. An image of Mr Curpep bounced back into his mind; for a moment he thought the man's face looked very much like the face of the great Trouser. 'Is this all a dream?' he said to himself, staring at the water just beyond his feet. 'Why does a thing like that have to bally happen? Now I'll never be able to take a friend to Trouser's party. I haven't got a friend.'

'AND BRING A FRIEND. AN AMALGAMATION OF TENTACLE IMPORTANCE.'

HO!
HE! HE
HA
HO HO!
HE HE!
PLEASE DANCE ON THE GRASS
ZIP!

HO!
HA
HA
HEEE
HA!
HE!

HA
HO
HO
WE
HO!
SNORT

HO HO!
GRAB
SHREDDD!!!

GUFFAW!
MUST BE GOING HE HE!
REND.

HA HA HA HA HA!
WHERE'S MY HAT!
SPLOONT!

PULL YOURSELF TOGETHER MAN! WHERE'S MY...
A BIGGER SPLOONT!

...HAT?

YOU'VE RUINED MY PANKING HOMBURG!

ANTI-TROUSERITE!
UGH!
SHRIEK!!

WILL I EVER FIND..

... A FRIEND?!
THE SWANS AREN'T REAL Y'KNOW!

The words rang in his mind like a bell.

Somewhere in the distance a swan honked and a clear female voice laughed joyously. Mr Straightly couldn't help feeling relaxed, though, after all that had happened. The park was so soothing. He stared down into the water and, for a moment, almost dozed off. He would have done so if it wasn't for the sun beating down on his head. He picked his hat up and placed it carefully on his red skull.

It was then that he heard a voice coming from the water.

'They're all artificial, you know,' the voice said in a thick Northern accent.

Mr Straightly started and looked up and there, about eight feet away, sticking out of the water, was a head.

'The swans. They're all artificial. So are all the birds here. The peacocks are artificial too.'

The head was definitely male, with a few black curly hairs, and a black moustache. It eyed Mr Straightly rather vacantly but it seemd friendly enough.

'Who the hell are you?' enquired Mr Straightly, rather snappily.

The being was moving closer and soon he was wading through the water, a slight smile coming from his buck teeth. He had long whiskers drooping out from the back of his moustache and the base of his nose. He looked very fishlike.

'I said, the swans.They're not real, you know. Oh, they look it, but you've just been feeding artificial swans. I expect you've done their circuits in with that nasty man's hat, not that I care, they don't interest me at all, not at all.'

He shook off the water and sat down beside Mr Straightly, who was amazed to see he was wearing a rubber suit that seemed to actually join his skin at the neck, hands, and feet. Mr Straightly thought it could no no harm to talk to the man, if man it was.

'Well, by jove.' He cleared his throat and gave his mousy moustache a scratch.

'I'd never have guessed, old chap. About the ah . . . swans, I mean. Artificial, eh? Never have guessed. Damn clever if you ask me. Ah, Straightly's the name, just Mr. How d'you do?'

'I'm fine, thank you, Mr Straightly, pleased to meet you. I'm Bruce, and I'm still evolving.'

'Well, hullo there, uh, Bruce, nice to see you, old chap.'

They shook hands and were friends instantly, although Mr Straightly didn't really understand that last statement.

'Tell me, where are you from, Bruce? How on earth do you do that water trick; gave me quite a nasty turn at first.'

Bruce answered delicately, almost with a lisp. 'I told you, Mr Straightly, I'm still evolving. I come from off the coast near Yorkshire; we had to start coming up on land. I tried to hijack a plane to take me to Cuba.' He looked at Mr Straightly with big, sad brown eyes. 'I been working in a casino. Do you want a cigarette? I've got a hundred in my pocket here.'

He produced some packets of large cigarettes. Mr Straightly said he didn't often smoke but he'd have one anyway. Bruce lit them with a match. He had to be very careful in case he burned his long whiskers. Bruce pulled on the cigarette.

'I . . . I just stole these. I walked into a bar for a drink and the barman wasn't around so I crept behind the counter and filled me arms with them. I dropped loads running away, though. He came out before I could get away and started spraying me with a soda syphon. I got soaked.'

'I . . . I just stole these. I walked into a bar for a drink and the barman wasn't around so I crept behind the counter and filled me arms with them. I dropped loads running away, though. He came out before I could get away and started spraying me with a soda syphon. I got soaked.'

Mr Straightly wiped the water from his eye which was still dribbling a little. The smoke from the cigarettes hung thickly in the warm air.

'I say, old chap, there's no need for that sort of thing in this day and age, surely?'

Bruce suddenly put his cigarette down and rushed into the water. For a moment he vanished completely and Mr Straightly thought he'd done something wrong and lost another friend. But soon some bubbles burst on the surface, and Bruce's strange head appeared like a black submarine surrounded by ripples.

'Sorry about that. I have to keep getting back into the water every now and again, not for long though. Could you pass me the cigarette please?'

The perpetually baffled Straightly handed Bruce his cigarette and stared with an expression of disbelief.

'You 'aven't tumbled yet, Mr Straightly, have you; don't you know what I am?'

'Well, er . . . no, I . . .'

'I'm a seal.'

'A seal?'

'Yes. A seal.' Bruce pulled on the cigarette and blew smoke rings out across the lake. 'Well, not completely a seal; I won't be one for much longer anyway. I'll soon be right out of the water, but at the moment I have to keep moist; I'll shrivel up otherwise. I rob banks; do you want to rob a bank with me? It's easy to do. You just walk in wearing a raincoat with your hand in the pocket and stick your fingers out straight, just tell 'em it's a gun . . . they always fall for it nowadays.'

'My goodness, Bruce, you are a character. There's no doubting that, bally interesting too, if you don't mind me saying so, but I'm not all with you on this seal bit. I . . . I mean, how did it happen?'

'It was you lot. You people, I mean; all that oil drifing around the sea and those nasty chemicals. I kept having nasty turns till one day it just got too much. I just floated to the surface and spewed up, it wasn't just me, we're all coming up now; it's all been polluted. I'll not hold grudges though, not me.

'I like it up here. I like stealing things. Not from people, of course, not from personal individuals; you know – big things. I'm gonna steal a bus and a saucerette and take it all to Cuba. Do you want to come with me?'

Mr Straightly looked with great interest at Bruce, who was now wading out of the still water, smiling gently and smoking his cigarette. He felt very sad for this poor creature, forced to leave the sea because of human idiocy and greed. It was just a passing thought; conscience was disappearing more and more every day now. Whatever happened, happened.

Mr Straightly looked intently at Bruce who, once more, sat dripping and grinning by his side.

'Look here, old chap, I admire a . . . ma . . . seal . . . er – fellow like you. I mean, not holding any grudges and keeping a stiff upper lip what-ho. How are you at parties? You've heard of the great Trouser, I take it?'

'Is it a kind of curry?' said Bruce.

'No, no, no, old chappie! Well, I can see I can help you as much as you can help me, if you'll pardon the expression. Music Therapy! The great one and only T.G. Trouser. Surely, you've heard about it? The greatest thing to happen since . . . well . . . since the workers' uprising of 1984. By jove, by golly, how long have you been on dry land anyway?'

Bruce threw his cigarette butt into the water. There were a few people crunching along the gravel path behind them; sometimes they would stop and look at the swans. Two or three had already sunk slowly to the bottom of the lake.

'I've been around a bit now,' said Bruce. 'Where's the party then? Will there be any good jumps there? I could do with a good jump.' Bruce grinned widely into Mr Straightly's face, his white buck teeth protruding slightly.

'Oh, what amazing good fortune! You'll come then? Marvellous, absolutely marvellous. Everyone will be there, old sport, just about everyone. Coming back for tea?'

'Have you got a bath? I might need one,' said Bruce.

Mr Straightly and Bruce got up to leave. Bruce lit up another cigarette and led the way along the edge of the blue lake and into a deep grotto with thick lush foliage hanging down around their heads. Mr Straightly was walking alongside Bruce through the maze of greenery when he noticed Bruce was limping slightly. He frowned and looked down at his own leg, the right one, and realized that Bruce was imitating him.

'You got a nasty limp there,' said the sealman. 'You ought to see a doctor about that, could turn septic, that could. Have you been and seen one?'

Before Mr Straightly could answer, a strange light flooded his vision. There was a loud 'pop', and the undergrowth disappeared. They seemed to be suspended in time and space for a moment, and then the light slowly dissolved and Mr Straightly found himself holding a bubble in his hand, about the size of a golf ball. It was transparent and had something inside it. He moved it closer to his eyes and found he was looking at a tiny landscape. There was a flesh-like wall surrounding a blue lake with a minute white line like a path running through green grass and patches of dark green dotted here and there along the bank of the lake.

'It's free, Sir,' said a woman's voice.

Mr Straightly and Bruce lifted their eyes and saw an old lady dressed in the manner of a fortune teller and smiling mysteriously.

'A souvenir of Electric City, Sir; goodbye.'

The two men looked at each other. Bruce grinned and shrugged and they both turned and walked out of the store. For a store it was, full of bric-a-brac, odds and ends of all description. They were soon out on the street and took a bubble chair back to Mr Straightly's apartment for tea, Mr Straightly rubbing his chin and frowning into the glass ball all the while. The ball was now absolutely clear.

Chapter 7
A Cow in Trouser House

London was vibrating nicely at 7.30 pm on Friday the 12th of June, the night of T.G. Trouser's Ball Party for Cabbages.

The great Trouser himself had been making preparations all day, organizing the entertainments which promised to be rich and varied, and a special consignment of exotic foods had just arrived at Trouser House. There were purple wasps in honey, blueberry pies, apples, oranges, bananas, pied sparrow on a stick, huge slabs of synthetic cheese, three-hundredweight of frozen Mongolian fly traps, three foot long monitor lizards ready for grilling, polluted squid curry, peppermint creams, pure hemp candy bars, boiled pine tree bark from the last five acres of pine trees in Almost Scotland. There were many barrels of wine in every colour possible, enough whisky to sink a battleship, and a real live cow. No one knew where Trouser had managed to get a cow from. They were considered not only obsolete, but probably a figment of the imagination anyway: but here indeed was a big golden brown cow, champing around in Trouser's house, eating bits of furniture.

The many assistants shook their heads and grunted when they saw the cow. They didn't know how one ate it. Does a cow taste better boiled or baked was the big question on everyone's mind. Or perhaps you just let it wander around and took chunks out of it at random; equip all the guests with a knife and fork. It all seemed a little uncivilized though.

Trouser, however, would not be bothered with silly questions on how best to prepare a cow, shaking his head and turning away. When anyone asked him he would say: 'Don't bother me with that; damn fools didn't send any instructions with it – use your imagination!'

Trouser busied himself with the visiphone most of the time, talking to various entertainers and musicians, making agreements over the fees and free Music Therapy they would receive. He sat in front of the visiphone and talked while a strange and beautiful lady curled his golden hair and another one, looking almost exactly the same, painted his nails. The Great Trouser was putting on weight around the stomach, and his face looked a lot bigger than usual. He realised people were beginning to notice, especially now, because of his apparent lack of interest in anything connected with Music Therapy. He could have easily taken that extra weight off with the right sound vibrations but he just didn't seem concerned. He had a strange gleam of new enthusiasm in his blue inward-staring eyes, and everybody thought that this party must be connected with something amazing and new about to occur in the history of Trouser.

They would be right too.

But perhaps only Mr Straightly had the deepest inkling, if only he could pull himself together long enough to think about it.

After most of the arrangements had been made, the slightly overweight Mr Trouser was faced with the task of deciding on what to wear for the party. He stalked out of his visiphone office followed by the make-up ladies who bobbed about, looking at him from all angles, making sure his nails flashed and his hair curled. When the door zipped open he was confronted by the cow who mooed loudly and shook her tail. Trouser pulled his face into a frown and looked down into the cow's big sad brown eyes, patting her head. 'Well, old boy, I can see you're going to be a bit of a hairy problem. That's for sure, you little rascal, you! But we'll have to give you a name, oh yes.' He walked slowly around the cow, scrutinizing her from all angles. 'Ah ha, yep. I see. Ah ha.' He sat cross-legged on the floor in front of her and went into a trance. The make-up girls stood as still as statues while the cow slapped her tongue in the air vacantly and dropped a pancake.

Suddenly T.G. Trouser bobbed up straight on his feet and, with his golden ringed finger, tapped the cow on the nose. His voice boomed.

'I name thee, great and noble fat cow from onlyTrouserknowswhere, "Three Points to the Home Team".'

The make-up ladies clapped their hands and a man standing a few yards away outside another door cheered happily. He wore a huge crinkly chef's hat and a white apron with blue and white checked trousers. He was thin and dark and sporting a pencil-line black moustache. 'Ah ha, sooo de Great Trouser has named the beastie, eh?' he said. 'Si si hombre, is a fine name, no? Come along zis way den little Three Points to ze Home Team, Pablo will see what he can doing.' The chef flashed a long carving knife and led the mooing cow away. Trouser looked on a little perplexed.

'I only hope he goes down well,' he said quietly.

Chapter 8
A Ball Party for Cabbages

The lights came on in Tint Street and in dribs and drabs people entered the main doors of Trouser House. Tint Street in fact consisted solely of Trouser House, being a tunnel-like affair which ran through the core of the building and ended in a pinpoint. The walls of the house were concave and rolled nicely around the tunnel with doors and windows which by eight o'clock were flickering bright and colourful light onto the plastic cobbled street.

At the very pinpoint of Tint Street, a strobolic light suddenly burst into life and pieces of glittering material fell from the ceiling, changing colour and shape. There were snake shapes, circles, smoke-ring shapes, shapes like the T.G. Trouser Music Therapy symbol; a blitz of sensual excitement created by 'the Archbishop of inner space', the tubby genius buffoon. He really knew how to toss a party, and this one was going to be a riot, perhaps even better than the last one, 'A Ball Party for Hare Fanciers', where Trouser had revealed the Imprint Cartoon machine, his latest invention – later to be called the 'Impcart T.G.T.', a marvellous device which allowed people who were having trouble with their time and space location whilst under Music Therapy to actually have a vision imprinted onto their inner eye of any reference within inner space. Some people found it very useful to help them find their bearings more easily once they were inside, not only for novices but for advanced explorers also.

It was even used in the permanently distracted ward for some really extreme cases, one of the first being a character of some worth and velocity who was just arriving at Trouser House. The Impcart T.G.T. had helped the man down to a more relaxed level where, occasionally at least, he could get a glimpse of a physical world reality. He would often argue that Trouser had saved him from a fate worse than life or, alternatively, he would say Trouser should have minded his own business. Whichever way his logic went, he was a likeable oddity.

He was Mr Bizarre.

The main door was wide open as the guests started to stream in. On the door, collecting the invites and watching out for suspect anti-Trousers were the Large Squad, One'ser, Two'ser, Three'ser, Four'ser and Five'ser, all dressed in electric blue suits with T.G.T. badges neatly shining on their lapels.

The music jingled out onto Tint Street and the guests were laughing wildly as the strobe and glitter shapes bombarded their senses. It was already apparent that this was going to be really crazy from the word GO as the people tumbled through the door and into the amazing Trouser Hall No 1 which, everyone remarked, reminded them instantly of an amoebic undersea existence.

The large room was dim, with tables and drinks liberally scattered, and liquid light bulbs suspended on thin wire moved around above the guests' heads hypnotically. Three or four gaily dressed people had already thrown off all inhibitions and were trying to catch the strange fish that swam in the wall.

Whether they were real fish or just projected images was uncertain but nobody was really interested in the mechanics of the situation; even when Dil and Dolse (who had arrived closely together) swore blind they had caught one.

The wine flowed freely as the place began to really zing, and everyone was speculating on what was going to happen next. There were sure to be some wonderful celebrities to appear at any moment, like Twiggott, for instance. He was bound to look absolutely amazing. 'And where was the genius Trouser, our host?' They all cried with delight – no doubt, ready, behind the scenes, for a big entrance.

The music, which was rich and illusive, and seemed to come from everywhere all at once, stopped abruptly. The chattering halted in mid-sentence, and a split second announcement was made in a deep bass voice. 'Follow the eyes please.' The music came flooding back rapidly, and everyone looked around expectantly as the wall at the back of Trouser Hall No. 1 slid open to reveal a dark tunnel full of large staring eyes, all different colours and sizes.

In went the crowd, poking the suspended, gleaming eyes, and laughing and cheering wildly; it was already getting a little hysterical. Just as the main doors were about to close, along came Bruce and Mr Straightly who were questioned by the Large Squad. Bruce looked at them with his buck-tooth grin and asked silly questions about their electric blue suits. His long whiskers were stiff and evenly spaced, and he wore a black coat and tails with a black bow tie and gleaming white shirt. Poor Mr Straightly was fumbling in his trenchcoat pocket for the invitation and getting rather nervous under the scrutiny of the Boy'sers who were impatient to shut the doors and mix with the crowd. Mr Straightly dipped his hand so deep into his pocket for the invitation, he toppled over into the arms of Two'ser, who was not pleased! Eventually the pair were admitted, and a Trouserite assistant took Mr Straightly's trench coat, thus revealing a natty pair of pressed light brown shorts with a subdued flower motif. They were rather overlong and his white legs looked remarkably thin and English underneath. Above, he wore an incongruously loud antique Hawaaian shirt. On his feet were a pair of thin brown plimsolls and matching socks just covering his ankles.

He looked ridiculous.

So did Bruce but it was, after all, a ball party for cabbages.

They followed the party down the tunnel of eyes, Bruce grabbing a glass of orange wine beforehand, the Large Squad close on their heels. The music grew louder as they neared the end of the tunnel and soon they could make out the shapes of the crowd popping out at the other end in a very brightly lit room.

When they were in the room (Trouser Hall No 2), Bruce and Mr Straightly realized what a truly magnificient occasion it was – the splendid array of guests all in their finest garb, and the food. They tucked straight into the purple wasps in honey and dunked their pied sparrow on a stick into a massive bowl of punch the size of a fishpond. In fact, Bruce was all ready to get in and have a little swim but Two'ser stopped him in time. Floating in the punch were at least two huge hemp plants and Mr Straightly was picking seeds from his teeth and laughing at everyone he saw.

'There's something in this punch,' said Bruce. 'You can't fool me y'know, I'm from up North; you can't get one past me. This punch is spiked with a drug!' He pronounced the 'u' in drug so deeply that Mr Straightly thought he was going to fall into the very word itself and never get out.

'I say, old chappie,' Mr Straightly said, looking conspiratorial. 'I say . . . have you ever seen anything like it before in your life?'

'Can't say I have; I could do with a jump though. Eh, can you see 'er over there, the one with the dead skinny neck and green skin? D'you reckon she does a jump, eh?'

Bruce's big mad idiot seal eyes were wide and spinning, he bit his bottom lip with his front teeth, showing bits of hemp stuck in between them.

'I know one thing, I might need a bath later on. I'm getting a bit dry under the arms; d'you think 'e's got a a bath somewhere in this place?'

Before Mr Straightly could answer, the music stopped and the guests, who were packed tightly together, fell silent.

There were vast chandeliers hanging from the ceiling reflecting a myriad of pattern across the hall, the walls were brilliant yellow, and the long polished tables stretched into an infinity of exotic foods.

Along to the left of Mr Straightly and Bruce were a series of tiny lights in the wall about six feet up, flashing green and red. All eyes were focused on the lights as the Large Squad asked everyone politely if they would move away from the wall. The music boomed back loud and rocking, and the excited crowd watched the space between themselves and the wall as if an apparition were about to appear out of thin air. Underneath the farthest flashing light a panel in the wall slid open and a cabinet inside it spun around to reveal a coffin-like perspex front, like a big test tube. And inside the tube, to the delights of the crowd, was the leader of the Large Squad and Trouser protector magnificent, Twiggott.

Twiggott stood behind the perspex, which slid open, bearing a wide grin. He wore thigh length tartan boots, almost mock astronaut at the bottoms, but covered with big silver and gold cobbles with blue stars in the centre. On his strong shoulders was a short stenolin black jacket with wildly exaggerated pointed shoulders and a bat-like collar. In fact, Twiggott looked like a giant vampire bat but for his customary turquoise mohican hair cut. Over his eyes was scarlet and indigo make-up, and his lips were a pale green with a blue spot on the bottom one, just slightly to the left.

He swaggered out of the cabinet holding a glass of green wine in one hand, and his silver cane slapped deep into his shoulder. The music was subdued for a second and the crowd were laughing ecstatically as Twiggott pointed down at his feet, obviously proud of his ridiculous boots. Some people were a little offended that above the boots he only wore pure white underpants. But this was only a passing whim.

Twiggott bowed low and strode into the crowd towards the punch bowl as the music came back louder than ever. The crowd shuffled together, talking excitedly and flashing glances at Twiggott who was dipping a glass into the punch bowl and stuffing his mouth with hemp. Mr Straightly had heard a little about Twiggott and gave him plenty of room. Bruce, however, could not restrain himself; he grinned and tapped Twiggott on the shoulder. Mr Straightly nudged Bruce and tried to warn him to be careful but the sealman ignored him. Twiggott, who was just about to take a long swig of punch, stopped the glass short of his mouth and slowly turned his head to face Bruce with a muted expression. Mr Straightly coughed and turned white from head to toe.

Bruce grinned and spoke: 'Ey, who the 'ell are you then?' His Northern accent was a little slurred; he seemed to be quite unaware of Twiggott's splendour and importance. 'You look as though you know yer way around this place; is there a bath in here, eh? I'm getting a bit dry around the feathers. I don't want to dry up completely or I won't be able to jump anything t'night.' Bruce grinned lecherously at the skinny woman with the green complexion. She winked and vanished into the crowd.

Twiggott held a tight gaze into Bruce's face. He took a sip of the punch and chewed a leaf of hemp as if it were gum.

'For a start, tooth features! If you don't know me name, you'd betta find out fast, then you'll know 'ow to address me proper. Right? Sayin' fings like that is liable to get yer 'ead cracked eggish. Understand?'

Twiggott glared at Bruce, twisting his cane around on his shoulder, and spat a hemp seed into his left eye.

Bruce lifted his hand up and rubbed the other eye. 'It's a good job you missed me good eye chuck. Eh, are you this Trouser fella, eh? Are you, are you the bloke who's running this show? Cos it's a right bloody laugh, innit, it's a right kettle of scaly fishes, eh?' Bruce giggled and looked around at all the people, some of whom were backing away, waiting for Twiggott to do something nasty.

There was no need to worry though, the fabulous Trouser protector was already joining in on the joke and considered Bruce harmless enough. He tapped the sealman elegantly on the head with his cane and told him to watch what he said in future. 'Lurk before you leap, wombie, or's you'll get stifled, quickish.'

Yet again the music died and everyone's attention was swiftly focused on another flashing light in the wall. People craned their necks to get a better view. A huge test tube spun around in the wall to reveal what at first appeared to be an Egyptian mummy wearing a long sequinned green and mauve robe. The face of the creature was white as snow and with mystical deity-like eyes. His hands were thin and white and the left one held a knobbly wooden walking cane which he leant on. The face of the tube slid open and out stepped (to rapturous applause) the one and only Mr Bizarre. While everyone's attention was on Mr Bizarre, who was strutting like a chicken in front of the wall, Bruce quietly slipped into the punch bowl and sank to the bottom. Flicking his robe behind him, Mr Bizarre looked at the ground with his black smiling eyes and occasionally flashed them up into someone's face in the crowd, giving them a strange sensual thrill. Back came the music and everyone converged in chatter and laughter. The food was gorged with great voracity and Mr Bizarre soon began digging into a grilled three foot long monitor lizard, its mouth stuffed with pieces of Yage bark. Mr Straightly didn't notice the disappearance of his friend. He found it incredibly hard to take his gaze from Mr Bizarre, who was doing a little performing with an infinity box.

The infinity box was a little toy Mr Bizarre had invented for children, but adults found it great fun too. He just held the box in his hand and pressed a hidden button, and, every time, something different popped out of it. First there was a bunch of artificial white flowers that shot out and showered people in the crowds; then there was a thirty foot long striped rubber snake; next came a flock of magnetic butterflies which stuck to the guests' jewellery and the metal food dishes; then there were a score of rubber dolls in the dumpy image of the great T.G. Trouser, bumping from wall to wall and richocheting into the crowd, closely followed by tiny beautiful paper models of almost every musical instrument known to mankind. This went on for some hysterical minutes and the room was littered with all manner of oddities before Mr Bizarre said, 'I thank you,' and bowed low. An infinity box had never been known to repeat itself. It was but one of the many fabulous inventions from the electric brain of Mr Bizarre, who had once been a leading show jumper before the 1984 workers' uprising. In his last contest he'd competed on the horse 'Eric Deric Third', and was approaching the last jump, a seven foot three brick wall; but as Mr Bizarre urged the horse to jump, something strange occurred. The animal jumped clean out of the stadium and landed in a nearby field, squarely, on all four feet, without apparent damage to horse or rider. Three people in the audience died of shock, and many others had to have medical treatment afterwards; Hampstead declared war on North Borneo, and the Prime Minister of England had a heart attack whilst using a whore – Gina Crude, a fat bitch who'd just painted her hair black and got her kicks by sticking steel pencils into people's eyes. Before renaming himself, Mr Bizarre had been known as Harvey something or other. No one could remember his surname.

After the amusing infinity box, the music again subsided, and a deep bass voice boomed, 'Follow the ears, please'. Which everyone did as they had done when the eyes appeared in Trouser Hall No 1. A few people could swear they heard a strange mooing sound as the voice spoke, but no doubt all would be revealed eventually.

Trouser Hall No 2 was left big and empty as the last man out, Mr Bizarre, glanced back at the giant punch bowl before entering the eerie tunnel. He thought he could see a stream of bubbles bursting on the surface of the liquid. He decided to investigate the phenomenon, reasoning that one didn't put bubbly champagne with a good punch, which it undoubtedly was. He skipped over to the bowl, surprisingly lightly for what must surely have been a very old man, and peered into the red and green depths. Out of his robe he pulled a stylish stainless steel pipe, filled it with his own concoction; dried yellow mutant ivy leaves, panama red hemp, pine needles, little pieces of wood chippings from an old chair that his grandmother had died in, and various other bits and pieces, and puffed contentedly, watching the little bubbles popping in the punch.

Presently, a head emerged grinning and looked up vacantly at Mr Bizarre who showed no surprise whatsoever but passed the pipe to the wet Bruce. Bruce puffed as he thrust a hand out for a lift-up. Mr Bizarre obliged and out came Bruce, wet and panting in the still, brightly lit hall. 'Ooph ee . . . ta mate, thank you very much, where did you steal that bowl of tripe from?'

Mr Bizarre assumed a rather mannered quizzical expression.

'Bowl of tripe. Pipe.' said Bruce. 'It's seal-jive. There's not much to do off the North coast in summer, so we used to invent little rhymes to pass the time, you know, like the cockneys who used to work on the boats sometimes. I pulled one of the daft buggers overboard once. I pulled on his net an' had him in the bloody sea! Then I went and bit his arse! Ha, I did! 'Oo the 'ell are you then, squire?'

Mr Bizarre put his pipe away and looked down at Bruce. He started speaking in a deep matter-of-fact voice. 'Ah ha, I was wondering when you lot would start coming up; you've taken far too long about it if you ask me. We're a load of wombats, you know, us human race.'

He produced his infinity box and shot a bunch of inflatable bananas across the room. He replaced the box with a small satisfied smile. Bruce's eyes followed the flying bananas before returning to Mr Bizarre.

'I'm still evolving,' he said.

'I'm devolving,' said Mr Bizarre soberly.

'Eee 'ow the 'eck do you do that then?'

'Oh, just a turtle trip really. Rather like a flying Amazon bedspread. First you jump the gaily spangled contemporary, then you pitch a wizard through a window. Quite easy really; just takes a little toe control.'

'You're a right one, I can see that,' said Bruce, pulling a strand of hemp from his wet sagging whiskers. 'Everyone's a bit queer in here if you ask me. God, I 'ope that's the last time I have to do a bit of wetting; I feel like a bloody dildo!'

'Well, for goodness sakes, Mr Sealish. This party wasn't really intended for the likes of me and you, no – surely, whether it be evolving or devolving, it still be far above the ilk of this little partisan rigmarole, eh?'

'The name's Bruce, chuck, after me father, God rest his rotting, polluted carcass.'

'Well, well, well, how do you do, Bruce? I'm the phenomenal Mr Bizarre, or if you wish, you may call me Bizer – all my close surrounding layers of eternity do. Oh, by the by,' Mr Bizarre threw a glance at the eerie tunnel in case anyone was about. 'I'm the only one here who knows what the tubby Trouser's wearing tonight.' He whispered low into Bruce's ear, trumpeting his rouged lips. 'He's wearing a wild animal trapdoor matinee jacket with a matching corset, and briar suspender underhangers, pimpled in the coarse equator desert stripping a silver forest underarm droplets with all but a gypsy tout picker.' He moved his long neck back and gave Bruce a gossip-like nod.

'Well, thanks for nothing, friend, what kind of English is that, eh? Sink the bloody Bismarck. 'Ave you ever robbed a bank eh? I need one, I do, I'm gonna rob a bank and take it to Cuba. Do you think I'll make a jump tonight, eh? I fancied a piece wi'green skin, dead skinny she was too; do you reckon on a jump here t'night, eh, d'you reckon?' Bruce looked up at the blank pale face of Mr Bizarre who turned like a slow robot and made for the tunnel, chicken strutting, followed by Bruce, who still looked very wet and not a little intoxicated.

In Trouser Hall No 3, everyone had taken their seats in what looked and felt like a smoky nightclub, complete with chandeliers, candelight, and dipping and bowing waiters all in tuxedos. There was a stage flooded with a warm red and blue light and people sat very near to it, chattering around heart-shaped wooden tables. Dil and Dolse had a little table all to themselves, and Dolse was all the while dropping strange poisoned words into Dil's ear. She was wearing an orange dress and so was Dil, but somehow whatever they wore, they still had the appearance of being in brown lab coats. They would have liked to have remained alone, at least Dolse would, but Mr Bizarre and Bruce had nowhere else to sit so they got two waiters to bring out two chairs and they joined the ladies.

'Perchance we drop our round hearts on stable cushions next to you, thank you greatly,' said Mr Bizarre to the girls, clasping his hands together like a vicar giving a sermon. Bruce sat down grinning at Dolse and trying to look down the top of her dress at her almost non-existent breasts.

'Hello, Mr Bizarre, I do like your robe. Make it yourself, did you?' Dil had adopted a very upper class party accent for the occasion – she'd been practising all week. Mr Bizarre flicked the sides of his robe and burst out laughing, staring up at the ceiling.

'He's a berk with an 'e', this fella,' said Bruce, leaning closer to Dolse, who was looking a little ill.

'Eh, 'ave you got any herring on you? I could do with a bit of raw herring. What's your name then, lover? I'm Bruce. I'm still evolving.'

Dolse immediately considerd Bruce to be a maniac or even a fish fetishist of some kind; there were a lot of them about lately. She leaned over and whispered something to Dil, flashing sly glances at both men. Mr Bizarre was by this time on his knees, giving the ample cheeks of Dil's bottom closer attention.

'Goodness, I don't know, I really don't,' she said. 'Do you always have to make an expedition out of yourself, Mr Bizarre; I mean, do you?'

'You, my dear lady, are starting to get a fair purchase on that bum stand. I shouldn't be surprised if you end up siliconed,' said Mr Bizarre, getting back on his seat and scratching his cheeks with a thin, bony hand.

'What?' said Dil, shaking her tubby breasts.

'Siliconed,' answered Mr Bizarre.

'Oo'er,' said Dolse. 'I 'ope that old Trouser gets appeared in a hurry, I'm getting bottled by this wet chap 'ere. Fancies me, I think ee does, Dil mate, hooo.' Dil and Dolse laughed into each other's eyes in their own very intimate way.

Bizer leaned over and said to Bruce, 'Keep your battleship in dock, wetlock, they're a remarkably smarmy pair and liable to bore you up your own orifice. He pulled out a giant pink plastic comb and ran it through his beige and battlegreen checked hair.

Bruce giggled when he saw that the hair changed to red, white and blue as the comb altered the style from a slight basin-cut to a prominent quiff.

The lights flashed on full for a split second and the words 'Trouser appearance' briefly settled the din of the party. There was a fanfare and all eyes excitedly surveyed the stage. A few people thought they heard a strange 'mooing' sound. A microphone rose from the stage floor like a snake being charmed; it was time for the genius buffoon host to make his exciting debut. Mr Straightly sat in a romantic candle-lit corner with the skinny green-skinned lady, who bobbed her head from side to side and used an animated smile like a beauty contest contestant. She said nothing and poor Mr Straightly, feeling a trifle conned and embarrassed, copied her every move. The Large Squad were looning around from table to table, and Twiggott sat in the middle of the floor with a fantastically beautiful lady all dressed in red fur. The exiled Dalai Lama had gone into a trance with his hand up the skirt of one of Trouser's make-up ladies. He said it was for religious purposes.

Wahin Tabloid McKnicker, the Chinese Scot born in India, was chain smoking atomic gorse bush cigars and completely On Holiday with two pads in his ears and one up each nostril. He kept trying to hold hands with Mr Tablet, who he thought was a mystical sun god. Mr Tablet politely refused, saying his reputation as a top level Music Therapist was at stake and anyway he didn't really go for that sort of thing.

Actually, Wahin was a little sad tonight as the character he was most anxious to meet was absent from the party. The man in question was a false Japanese dwarf known as Mr Slit-Bong Hi-Kids who had designed the Holiday Pods, Vacation Plugs or 'Vacos' as they were frequently referred to. Trouser himself had hired the services of Hi-Kids after having a massive brainwave relating to an idea concerning pocket M.T. devices. Realising a mind-altering sound device could be miniaturised he soon found the perfect man for the job in the brilliant diminutive dwarf. Within a few short years the pods were used and abused by one and all, the perfect way to adjust the day.

The fanfare was rather overlong and tedious but eventually the lush red curtains, with a gold T. G. Trouser symbol curled open. There was almost complete silence when the ridiculous Trouser emerged, riding the cow, 'Three Points to the Home Team', his golden curly hair sticking out under a see-through fez with a multi-coloured tassle swinging from the top. He wore a beautifully fitted silver suit which almost hid his portliness and a lime-green shirt with golden fish tie. He grinned like a clown and, behind the cow, a small boy cracked the whip to urge the beast forward. Trouser was really happy but had a nagging feeling that the cow was going to take him off the end of the stage and into the audience, for audience they were, and loving every minute of it. Tremendous applause threatened to shake the very foundations of the buiding and Trouser, jubilant and intoxicated by the response, kicked the cow in the ribs with his 1960 Chelsea boots, waving a hand in the air and blowing kisses. His round blob-like face and vacant but magnetic eyes looked remarkably comical above the mooing cow who had reached the end of the platform and was lolling her tongue over the edge at the crowd.

CRACK!
I'VE HAD..
ENOUGH!
PLOP!
?
SPLAT!!!
SWINGGGGG
WHOOOOPS!
ZOOM!
CRASH!
WHO'S GOT BONEY KNEES?!
HERE!!
CRACK!
SUCK
SUCK

Trouser, believing he had the cow under control, went completely haywire and bounced up and down rapidly lifting his fez on and off, grinning hysterically. He suddenly realised how much he'd missed his charming ego. He circled the cow skilfully round and round the stage, just missing the microphone by inches, until disaster struck. The cow, after revolving at least twenty times, became a little fed up with the whole thing. As they did the last revolution, the cow teetered dangerously near the edge of the platform. A few people gasped but Trouser remained elated and oblivious of any possible mishap. Three Points to the Home Team gave a giant shrug and flipped her rider sidelong into the air, where he spun twice and landed on a table with his legs skywards and his glass fez jammed over Dolse's thin astonished face. Bruce made an instinctive dive under the table, and Dil made a grab at the fez trying desperately to yank it from her bosom friend's face. Mr Bizarre repeated endlessly the words, 'By Christ, there's been an air raid! By Christ, there's been an air raid!' He said it with great conviction.

Trouser, still unable to fully grasp what had happened, fell off the table bringing it down with him with a loud crash. Poor Dolse went berserk and rushed around the guests, pulling at the jammed fez. She was rapidly running out of breath, and looked a little dangerous until the resourceful Twiggott took charge of the situation. He gripped Dolse at the back of the neck and shouted, 'Anyone 'ere got bony knees? C'mon 'urry up fer fucks sake, le's 'ave a look at yer knees.'

Mr Straightly bounded forward, and Twiggott pushed Dolse down level with the man's bare white knees. 'Knee potential, tha's wot you got, boy'ser, knee potential. Now if we can jus' crack dis fez eggish like, we's be well away, eh?'

'Certainly old chappie, ah . . . um, bally well let me at it, I'll save the day,' said Mr Straightly in deadly seriousness. He brought his knees together with a loud crack and the fez fell to pieces. Dolse pulled in a deep relieved breath, her black eyes stared wildly at nothing. It was a stroke of genius typical of the sort of magical events that surrounded Trouser.

The party was back in full swing again. A troupe of musicians appeared, playing wildly as they strolled through the crowd like wandering minstrels. Bruce stayed under the table and fell asleep, dreaming of the sea.

Trouser was back on stage holding the microphone, his silver suit spotlighted, and a long glass of yellow wine in his hand.

'And now, ladies and gentlemen. May your stimulated attention please plank itself on the wild idiot musicians now strutting the floor. They, dear people, are a wonderful bunch of staunch Trouserites like yourselves, and shall be announced as follows.'

Waiters rushed around with plates of meat and forks for the guests.

'Oh, by the way,' continued Trouser, 'the most honourable beast "Three Points to the Home Team" is, in factuality, a thing called a cow.' There were astonished cries from some members of the audience.

'Yes . . . incredulope as it may sound. A cow. Ahem, we were thinking of serving him as a light snack for your enjoyment, ahem. But difficulties arose as to the best way of serving him up.' Trouser suddenly broke into a feminine stance, complete with limp wrist and faggish facial expressions. 'Mm . . . we didn't know what to do to honeyrose, mm . . . should we souse the little sweet or fry him? Oh, look at me, tch tch, gone all weak in the knees I have, mm.' The people roared with laughter. 'Mm yes . . . or we thought perhaps we'd grill him with a little bit of horseradish and celery, mm . . . tasty.' They all fell about laughing, Trouser made another identity detour, this time as a sort of American salesman figure.

'Well, we just thought, like-a, we'd leave the old fella to graze a few more years before he makes that ole happy grunting grounds in the sky, ya'll understand? So . . . we cooked the chef instead, Pablo. Hope ya'll enjoy him!' He danced off the stage, blowing two-handed kisses saying, 'Back in a minute, honey's, back in a minute.'

Everyone agreed that Pablo was quite done to a turn; Gina Crude almost choked on a piece of his hat. She deserved to.

The musicians were in full swing, prancing around in the crowd and getting them to join in with handclaps and choruses. They broke into a very funky instrumental and suddenly Trouser was back on stage.

'It's me. Yes, me again,' he said with a grin.

He jumped down onto the bright blue floor. Taking the lead from the musicians he strolled through the crowd holding the microphone.

'Well alright alright alright alright alright,' sang the singer, a tall, token negro with close cut hair and triangular shades.

'Shake dat finger, let it cook,
here come here come Rodney Shook!
O yeaaah,' he sang.

Trouser waved a hand in the general direction of the singer and announced him. 'And on vocal chords and assorted grunts, we have the expressionable, the soul fiend, the magnificent, the Holiday-eyed, the Falling Parrot-like, the damn silly – Mr Rodney Shook!'

'Hurrah,' said the guests. The music rocked and rolled.

'Now don't point dat pickle, or throw dat yam,
everybody know I am what I am,
I'm Rodney Rodney Rodney Shook.
Now make it cook cos I'm really, really, shook,
Whowyeeah . . . uh.'

'Thank you, Rodney, a free heavy wet jungle juice Music Therapy course lasting for six months goes to you, and I must say, ya'll sure do need it,' continued Trouser. 'And on violin, Mr Violin-Smile.'

Mr Violin-Smile was attired in gypsy type clothes and played a colour-changing instrument, he did a quick soulful solo which everyone loved. Some people had jumped onto tables as the players performed; Bruce slept on.

'And on electric guitar, the world famous, the innovator, the slim and phallic, the best in the world . . . Mr Dirk Stick, let's hear it for Dirk!'

Dirk Stick thrust the penis-shaped guitar between his thighs, and blew a ripping piece of twelve bar blues. Mr Straightly was on a table standing right next to the amazing guitarist and looking round and round for the amplifiers – where was the sound coming from? The lights were unbelievable.

'And on electric portable organ and piano . . . a big hand please for Mrs Ina Freedom; and on bass, the strolling, the bloody Heavy, the man they used to call "Hold the panking walls up Charlie!" The greatest basso profundo in the whole multiverse! Mr Heavy String!!'

He was a remarkably fat man with a black bulldozer beard and tiny twinkling eyes. He made everyone's crutch vibrate when he played.

'And last, but not least . . . the man with the long blond hair and mug of ale. On percussion, Mr Paul After-Hours-Incidents!! Let's hear it please, give the boy a big artificial hand; that's the way; great boys all of them!'

Mr Paul After-Hours-Incidents was one person, at least, who was hoping the party would be a long one.

The band pranced their way to the stage where they performed the new 'Head and Shoulders Symphony' written by Rodney Shook, who, after a shaky start, had the audience in the palm of his hand. T.G. Trouser joined in on a few old farourites and Twiggott had a go himself. He was a gentle ballad singer and surprised most people with his warm sensitive voice. The time, what was left of it, was getting late. Outside the sun was trying to break through some miserable grey clouds. Some guests were being carried out and taken home, others had had orders to stay. Trouser carried a little brown bag with him and in the bag were several white badges with words printed on them. He handed them to certain guests and told them to wear them. 'Hang around with Trouser' the badges proclaimed, and Mr Straightly was very proud to receive one although he had to say goodbye to the green-skinned lady; she didn't get one. Bruce, who had awakened at last and was deep in conversation with Mr Bizarre and a few others, had got his badge neatly pinned to his lapel. This was really the whole point of The Ball Party for Cabbages – to bring the likely candidates for a new Trouser phase together.

'Aha . . . Mr Straightly, old horse! How are you feeling?' said Trouser, chewing on a pied sparrow and drinking punch.

'Gad. Bally topping, Mr Trouser, sir. Splendid do! Absolutely top hole, what!'

'Good. Glad you stretched your knees to the occasion. Now, if you'll walk this way – not literally, of course – we'll introduce you to some other possible expeditionaries, seeing as you've been rather busy all evening trying to get your plimsolls down that woman's plastic titty suspenders, eh? Naughty, naughty. Straightly, Straightly! C'mon, thisaway, Señor.' Trouser winked at the baffled Mr Straightly and led him to a table where Bruce was sitting. 'In the red corner, we have Mr Bizarre, or Bizer as he is sometimes referred to, Mr Bizarre – Mr Straightly.'

'I say, ah actually, we have met before, Mr Trouser, sir, am I not correct, Mr Bizarre?' Mr Straightly motioned for a handshake.

'I refuse to commune at present, perslap the ear of this reference piece I am in deep time fix with Mr Fish,' said the pale Mr Bizarre with an intent gaze into Bruce's eyes.

'The name's Bruce, chuck, Bruce . . . eee by Christ, this one's a right berk with a capital 'E' this one is, Mr Straightly, in't you, eh? Bird-features! This bloke, Mr Straightly, 'e thinks we're living in the molecule of a lobster! In a bloody lobster, for Christ sake! 'E don't believe me when I say that all the lobbies as we used to call 'em; all the lobbies are crammed together in the Sargasso Sea trying their hardest to breed with the eels. They reckon – they reckon that's the only way they're going to pass through the next evolution crisis.' Bruce thrust his teeth forward and broke out from what had been quite a serious expression for him, into his usual idiot grin. 'Eee bloody daft, is right, mate! Mating with the bloody eels, Christ, chuck, it's 'ard enough trying to screw a cod when you're 'ard up, but a bloody eel . . . he, Christ !!!' He laughed for a while before rushing off to be sick.

Twiggott crossed the dim floor towards them, casting a suspicious look after Bruce. Mr Straightly scratched his head.

'Aha ahem, Twiggott, my good man,' said Trouser, 'you were in good time tonight, stick wid me kid and you'll wear tin cans; you've met Mr Straightly, of course.'

'Sort of,' answered Twiggott, taking off his green mohican hair cut and examining it. He frowned when he saw the slight crease it had acquired during the course of the party.

'I tell you what, boss, dat seal ought to watch 'is tone control, 'e don't act standard dat wombi, das fer sure.'

'Oh he might come in useful yet you know, when the mission starts,' said T.G. Trouser, his mouth watering slightly. 'Ah, here come a few friends I think you'll be seeing a lot more of in the near future, Mr Straightly.'

He changed to an Australian accent.

'Jeez, what a pair youse are, you look like you've had yer heads under a

barrel organ all night. Watch out for these two Sheilas, Straightly, they're as close as Siamese twin bushbabies – meet Dil and Dolse, a remarkably smarmy pair'

Mr Straightly tried to smile but found it difficult.

Dil and Dolse giggled and stood very close together. Standing behind them was a small man. Mr Straightly hadn't noticed him at first but now he saw he was wearing a kilt. Definitely a man of taste, thought Mr Straightly. 'Ah, I say, Mr Trouser, sir, who . . . who is that chap? The ah . . . one wearing the kilt.'

Trouser gestured to the man to come out from behind the ladies. 'A fine bonny bundle this one, Mr Straightly, let me tell you. A real sandwich character. This man . . . THIS MAN,' he bellowed and made Mr Straightly jump, 'IS . . . the finest brain engineer since the cave man era. He will be of great importance to this dubious mission we are all about to overtake. I'd like you to meet the one and only, Duffy Wigman.'

Duffy Wigman curtsied gingerly. He wore a kilt with a gigantic black sporran hanging down, like a dead animal. His sturdy legs were graced with long pillar-box red socks and black shiny army boots. On his head, neat and trim, grew soft red hair. His small face had a rubbery weatherworn appearance and his teeth were rather yellowish. He adjusted his green military style jacket, and addressed Mr Straightly.

'How do ye do, Mr Straightly, can ye no get into the light where I can git a proper look at ye; ya look a bit on the pale side, a ye areeght?'

Duffy Wigman spoke with a broad Scottish accent.

'Bally well never felt better, thank you Mr Wigman, sir, pleased to make your acquaintance. Where did you get the smashing sporran from?'

'Ach weel, this was a wee present from ma last sexual encounter; d'ye really enjoy it that much?' He reached his freckled hands down and lifted the sporran. 'Weel, can ye no latch on to what it is? The wee canny thing is made entirely of pubic hair, aye, the whole bloody object! I personally have made a life study o' the subject, aye, and it's nae all female either, let me tell ye.' Duffy Wigman winked at Mr Straightly and looked down at his khaki shorts for a brief moment.

'Well, that's bally interesting, if you don't mind me saying so, Duffy old bean. A craftsman you must be indeed,' said Mr Straightly with blinding enthusiasm.

'Okay, is everybody 'appy?' said Trouser, 'I do believe it's time for the Bed Room.' Trouser led the remaining guests to a door and ushered them through. Behind the door was the bedroom, and what a sensational bedroom it was too, for it consisted entirely of one massive bed. Just cushions and sheets and blankets and alarm clocks and mirrors and ashtrays. There was a large glass bowl full of Vacos in the centre of the bed and everyone took a little Holiday before they climbed together into the bed.

The Ball Party for Cabbages was over. Outside, the rain piddled down.

Chapter 9
Trouser makes another Improbable Speech

The next morning saw T.G. Trouser up at the crack of dawn, waltzing around in a flurry. He wore his soft pink important speech-making suit and set about arranging Trouser Hall No 3 just so, while his select guests slept on. Sadly, Trouser's elated mood was subdued by what he called an ill omen.

When he was standing on the stage practising his speech, his cow, Three Points to the Home Team, collapsed in a heap in front of him after he'd only uttered a single sentence. She grunted loudly, farted, and shot forth a stream of urine, her big brown eyes looking appealing into the pale blue eyes of the genius Trouser.

Trouser was annoyed. He leapt from the stage, clear over the fat beast and commenced to dance around her, swearing loudly.

'You're a turd! Why why why? Why do you have to do this to me? What is the meaning of this outburst? I suppose you know this is an ill omen, friends, do you?'

Trouser shook an accusing finger at the animal who just lolled her red tongue on the dark floor. Suddenly the man understood the trouble. He noticed the cow's massive sagging tits, they'd definitely swollen since yesterday – her udders were bloated tubes of red flesh.

'Of course,' he said, as three Trouser assistants milled around, brushing his jacket and fluffing around his curly golden hair. 'If only the bastards had sent instructions with the blessed thing. What the hell do they expect, farming tactics? Quick, pluck the nipples.'

The assistants, two girls and one sort of man, bent over and pulled at the beast's paps.

'Not like that, not LIKE THAT!' shouted Trouser in a fluster. 'Have you never heard of the law of gravity?' He spoke with a German accent. 'Pull za creature's legs up into za air and squirt za miluk skybound, achtung! Or similar.'

They followed his instructions and up shot streams of white milk, hitting the lumpy ceiling and spilling back down onto the cow and the assistants. Trouser raised his hands to the air as if he'd just created rain. The cow, Three Points to the Home Team, positively smiled in relief. Mr Straightly stumbled into the room and tripped on a stool, falling loudly on the floor. A great day had started.

They were all there, Mr Bizarre in a white T-shirt with 'curtain thinker' printed on it, and thick baggy navy blue trousers. On his feet he wore Chinese Mandarin shoes with huge curly ends hooking around on themselves. He sat staring at the stage, a white-faced clown in the audience. He was thinking about trees which bore people instead of fruit. Bruce had his arm around Dilly who giggled and kept looking at Dolse, who was tight-lipped and a little annoyed. Bruce was drinking a glass of water. Mr Straightly was in quite a state altogether, he'd managed to burn one of his gingerish eyebrows lighting a cigar for Duffy Wigman. He had a bandage over it and was working up a nice little anxiety about how best to remove it with the least pain. His moustache was looking extraordinarily limp; indeed his whole appearance was of a starving, disease-ridden, retired colonel. His nervous twitch had reappeared with great vigour, and his knees ached. The only thing that kept him hanging on was the thought that he had finally left the world of his old Auntie Paperclip, and entered with dashing ferocity the sublime circles of society and something big was in the offing – that was certain.

Trouser took the stage in his pink suit and gave a little cough. He spoke through the microphone at first but it was so loud that it hurt everyone's ears and so he decided on a more intimate approach.

'Well, friends, colleagues, protectors, dubious bird imitators, etc. etc., I have gathered you all together in one fell swoop not just for a party, not just for a swollen think machine experience . . . NOT just for a quick leg over with Gina Crude . . . but for a large event. An event likely to change the future course of the whole Third World, a ridiculous experiment which will doubtless be my downfall, and thus, the rest of the world's too; who cares? You only live a few billion times. Watch out for the tadpole trap, friends, I say it again. Beware of the dead spot between metamorphosis, for the time has come like so many other people here tonight, d'you understand?'

It was obvious nobody did. Twiggott clapped, Bruce grinned and whispered something into Dilly's ear, and Mr Bizarre pretended to be dead.

'To put it simply and flatly, friends!' Trouser bellowed; 'To put it in a 3-D hatstand, we, and believe me you should think yourselves lucky in this, are going on a little journey to the stars. We are going to break this Music Therapy inner space cycle and get back into outer space, up, into the great beyond.' He stood with arms and eyes raised to the ceiling. A tiny blob of milk mixed with condensation dripped down onto his nose.

Mr Straightly applauded and uttered ridiculously extravagant appraisals. Bruce grinned and said 'Eeeee, daft bugger's lost 'is bonce, if you ask me.' He said it very quietly for the Large Squad were sitting behind him, each one of them looking fed up. Duffy Wigman was the most attentive, he'd been waiting for something like this to happen for years. He was desperately hoping it wasn't a joke.

Trouser continued, 'We shall begin the Beguine in three days from now, armed with amphetamine and nutron pills; we shall journey via saucerette to what used to be called India and from thence overland, by foot even if need be.'

Rodney Shook screamed, 'Oh, yeeah baby.'

'Now,' said Trouser after sitting down on the edge of the stage. 'Are there any questions?'

'Yeah, what the 'ell are ya on about, boss?' said Twiggott, adjusting his bat collar. 'I mean, are ya really gonna leave Music Therapy an' all, jus' like that, I mean, can we survive if we goes on dis little journey, sponk to the rest of 'em, can WE make it wivout regular treatment? Oh yeah, an' why is you puttin' on so much weight recentwise like?'

'Well, Twiggott, to answer the last part of your question first. I'd like to show you my sagging stomach bag.' Trouser pulled his shirt out and revealed an overlarge tummy. 'Look at it', he said. 'I could have reduced it to a mere nut with vibrations, could I not? But recenty I have been so pissed off with the very idea, I just don't give two sponks, three even. I mean, do you remember, Twiggott, the day I managed to spike the tap water under the Houses of Parliament with millions of different coloured prawns just to prove it could be done? What the hell! When I move, baby, I move with both feet.' Trouser's square body shook with fervour. 'Yes, Twiggott, I know what I'm doing, even if I don't, I mean, Christ, this is the big one, you gotta get your kicks, right?'

'Oh yeah, baby,' screamed Rodney Shook.

'Look,' Trouser said, dropping off the stage and spreading his hands; he was starting to enjoy himself.

'Apart from the general boredom, I mean apart from the whole rut-like rigmarole of sound excursions, what's so wrong with illusions anyway? C'mon, you tell me. Look if we flash off into outer space or similar, how is it going to screw the karma straightwise? We're all to blame anyway. I mean now we can come back and really use the ole cycle. Yeah? We can really use the ole body strut. Not like the wombats in 1970 did, not in that half-hearted is it a head phase or is it a body phase fashion. I mean really appreciate the cell of the situation, d'you understand? Apart from that, of course, there's the exploding men.'

There was silence in the hall. All eyes were on the performing Trouser. He looked a jewel; even Mr Bizarre was taking some interest, although somewhat intermittently.

'Did you say exploding men?' asked Four'ser, chewing a matchstick.

'That is indeed, almost the crutch of the matter, in fact, if I wasn't so damn clever, it would be the heart, soul and orifice of the matter,' answered Tee Gee Trouser.

'Ah dinna ken,' spluttered Duffy Wigman, hands on sporran.

'Exploding men? To cut a long story bigotedly short, these exploding men can apparently walk into any departmental store or similar, dressed in clean trendy suits and sink-into-the surroundings-type haircuts, complete with boring everyday slightly behind the high tuning persons version mouth patter, and explode, unexpectedly. They just explode. Blow the whole panking place up. Deadly bastards. Can't figure out a warning system yet. No doubt some bright boffin will soon, may be you, Duffy Wigman, if you could stop concentrating on that sporran of yours for a wee mo.'

'Ma God, Trewser, that's dastardly, och, a wee bit on the fiendish side, don't ye think?' Duffy was obviously annoyed at the very thought of exploding men.

'Yes, I'm afraid so, I've been putting my feelers out in more ways than one. Jerry Can and Toni the Cortina are one thing, exploding men . . . tricky business,' he scratched his jaw and looked at the ground.

'If de've got anyfing to do wiv dese 'ere explodin' men, I shall crack da pair of 'em eggish final, das the truth, boss, I means it!' Twiggott was raring to go.

'No, No, No,' said Trouser, with a wave of his stubby hand. 'Not sharp enough, those boys, not sharp enough. Not enough pieces for them to pick up afterwards. Not even so much as a lung left lying about after these exploding bastards get in. The whole show goes up, whoosh. It's no joke, I can tell you, somebody's after me and it's not just J.C. and Toni the Cortina. Who knows, they might even be an independent rebel movement. A mutation, appearing in time to save the world from a fate worse than Trouser. More Trouser.'

Everybody laughed, thinking the joke immensely funny, only T.G. Trouser frowned. He looked a little uneasy; it wasn't surprising really. Things had been building to a head recently, in more ways than one.

'Yes, I think we are ready for a newish Electric Jesus,' said Mr Bizarre in a cracked robot-like voice. 'Not for a moment doubting your obvious genius, of course, Trouser, but I think a little bit of . . . vast electric suspension could do us all the world of good. I mean, this tub has been scraped rather overlong, who knows . . . perhaps even an exploding messiah, instantly disposable, oblivion all round.' He rubbed his hands together and grinned fiendishly, he was into a down space at that moment and was almost talking sense for once.

Trouser spoke, 'Well, we're all agreed then. In three days time we embark on a major non-inside expedition. Out to the hidden country that has been kept a closely obscured secret for so many years, for there lies our destiny, in an antiquated but efficient space capsule bound for the outer vision, the large physical illusion. Would anyone like a drink and a whore?'

Chapter 10
Trouser accosts the Exploding Man

It might have been safer for all concerned if the Trouser party had left for their destination on that very morning after; instead certain things had to be taken care of. Trouser was to tour Central Music Therapy with Twiggott and a couple of the Large Squad to elect a new head of Music Therapy. It wouldn't be a difficult matter, the business seemed to take care of itself with or without Trouser these days. He was, however, a powerful image of security for most of the world's population, so some kind of passable replica had to be maintained. A group of mad artists, scientists, and plastic surgeons were hired to build a lifelike robot for TV appearances, public speeches, etc. It would keep the whole thing together for a few more years at least.

One'er, Two'ser, Twiggott, and Trouser were blimping around the vast complex of Central Music Therapy in bubble chairs that morning, 24th July, 2073, doing a little survey. The Great Trouser had just elected a new head, someone who could carry out the basic sacred Trouser duties without anyone having to know the difference. He was a highly advanced music therapist who had studied the Trouser style for years. He was so happy when Trouser elected him that he blurted out, 'By Jove, it must be a psychic beverage,' a phrase made famous by Mr Bizarre when they found him standing in a plastic hedge, on a raft, floating down the inner London canal two summers ago.

The man/woman elected for the job was, of course, the famous transvestite and timber fancier, Mr Anyquestions Mrs?, a being to be watched with both or more eyes.

'I think Mr Anyquestions Mrs? will be just the man for the job, Twigg, don't you? A real dazzle caricature if I ever saw one, a real Sombrero freak, eh?'

'Oh yeah, boss, 'e's awright, bit on the kinky side fer sweepin' de floor anyway; I wouldn't chuck it outa bed meself, not fer a brass club to crack anti-Trouserites eggish, I wouldn't, know wot I mean, boss?'

'Certainly, Twigg, my velly good man, you speakum with forked tongue, something velly much to my liking.'

Trouser was in the Centre Point food and drink hall with Twiggott and One'ser and Two'ser. They were sipping soya soup from silver flasks and lounging in bubble sofas, loking out of the window across the rooftops. If you stood up, you could just see the pleasure dome of Piccadilly Circus, this being the top floor of C.M.T. They continued with the light conversation for some while until Mr Tablet approached with another man beside him. Tablet was wearing a natty orange pin-striped number with lime green patch pockets and a white handkerchief spotted with blood.

'Oh hello, Mr Tablet, my good excuse for a man, how are all the patients in deep spinal experience Ward Ten these days? Really zombied, I hope?' Trouser smiled amiably as he looked up at Mr Tablet.

'Oh zooming, zooming, Mr Trouser, sir, absolutely. How's the inspection going along? Oh yes, and thanks for the wonderful ball party for cabbages, really inner space, the whole thing, really inner space! By the way, I'd like you to meet a new patient of ours, he's quite a phenomenon. Do you know, we put him into a deep Bach distortion trance the other day and he came out of it convinced that it was a Strauss waltz. Gnats' piss for the masses. Amazing, isn't it? Still suffering from the twentieth century piffle trauma. One in a million I'd say, at least.'

'Umm, you could be fractionally right, Mr Tablet, fractionally.' Trouser threw a glance at Twiggott who was buffing one of his mock astronaut boots. Twiggott knew the look well; he knew Trouser was suspicious of Mr Tablet's companion.

Trouser's astute mind was clicking over the details – average height, boring trendy appearance, stupid tasteless lemon shirt with a mass-produced sleeveless jumper under a thin, wide check suit. Cloggy two-tone shoes, sink into the background type face with multi-boring dark brown haircut. 'No pretence about the man whatsoever; must be something a bit bee-track here,' thought the genius Trouser. 'No style about the man, looks as if he's about to get married tomorrow or something equally dumb; I'll question him subtly.'

'Sẽnor, pleased to cross your universo, your name and meal-time preference please.'

'Um, me, oh yes . . .' said the man.

'I'm Mr Straight'n'Nasty, and I'll have a plate of greasy potato pills if you have any.'

'Tell me, Mr Straight'n'Nasty, how do you make friends? Throw a sort of prove-yourself-to-be-one-o'-the-gang type ritual? Throw a party-smarty line?' Trouser was being cute. The stranger was obviously a little flustered, almost a big flustered, in fact.

'Uh . . . a jest I take it.' The man laughed nervously and fumbled in his average pockets.

'Jest? Jest WHAT?' said Trouser, waving his tubby hand alarmingly in the air.

'Jest . . . jest,' said the man, putting on some black horn-rimmed glasses.

'Don't try to confuse me!' said Trouser, getting to his feet. 'Have you got a code phrase, Mr Straight 'n' Nasty, eh, a code phrase? Let me put it another way, if you'll excuse the expression, do you go off with a bang when the location has been established? Are you trying to explode?' Trouser pointed at the man, his dumpy finger amazingly close to the man's eye, his legs apart defiantly. Twiggott had decided to get his phial of Gripping Scab ready, just in case he had to shoot it over the man's face to make him lose his bearings. The Centre Point food and drink hall emptied in a flash.

'Look, I don't know what you're talking about; exploded! It's ridiculous,' said the man.

'Precisely!' said Trouser. With that, he leapt forward, grabbed the man by the scruff of the neck and threw him out of the window. Twiggott, One'ser,

Two'ser, T.G. Trouser, and Mr Tablet leaned out of the window to watch the descent.

He hit the rubber pavement with a smack, they could see it change colour rapidly. The man, however, did not explode, his guts were splattered all down the street. A solitary scream reached the Trouser party's ears. They slowly moved away from the window. Trouser frowned and looked a little pale. He spoke carefully.

'A nice sort of chappie, was he, Mr Tablet? Apart from the obvious, of course.'

'Yes he . . . ah . . . was okay, you know, okay.'

'Yes, unfortunate that, damn unfortunate,' said Trouser. 'Felt sure the bastard was about to explode at any minute, he looked the part, all the way. Bloody unfortunate . . . still . . .' He cleared his throat and motioned towards the door, 'Must press on.'

Mr Tablet suddenly looked anxious. He motioned for them to stop and flashed frightened glances from one to the other. 'Wait . . . wait!' he said. He broke down and started sweating profusely. He was wearing a mauve jacket with white shirt, and fawn, trendy, bum-tight trousers. His hair was a trifle too nondescript for the customary Tablet flair; he was usually a dashing therapist with a Mickey Mouse T-shirt.

Trouser's astute mind clicked over the details, he and the Large Squad took new interest in Mr Tablet, they eyed his appearance with almost disbelief. He looked back at them appealingly and rather pathetically as he spoke.

'Now I . . . look, I . . . I don't know how to put this; but I've been through a change . . . a metamorphosis, you know ah . . . something's happened.' He picked through the words uncertainly; he looked like a man suddenly having to find an excuse for his very existence, and having to spout it out to everyone, to exorcise his fear of being what he was.

Trouser trembled slightly and then spoke: 'Mr Tablet, my good friend and colleague, don't do anything I might regret later. This . . . this attire you're decked up in, surely just a ruse? You haven't forsaken Mickey Mouse, have you? I do believe you're having one of your little jokes, Mr Tablet eh, aren't you?' It was obvious Trouser was rankled by the situation. He expected the worst.

'How did it happen then, Tablet, old pill? C'mon, you can tell the ole Trous' hey baby?' He tried to sound amiable and failed. The tension was mounting steadily.

'I'm sorry everyone, I'm sorry. As you've obviously surmised, I'm an exploding man, watch me closely.' He stared at them miserably.

'B . . . but how?' said Trouser with some exasperation. 'Quick, tell me the details! I want to know the name of the tailor, the code number, the fitting department manager's name, address and bedside phone combination. Come on, Tab, lay the sandwich on me, just for old times sake!' He sounded urgent.

'Yeah, c'mon babe, don't go an' explode on us fer panks sake, ya can't do it ta yer old closeknits, can ya eh?' said Twiggott.

Mr Tablet clasped his hands around his own throat. 'Sorree, you'll have to do a Straight'n'Nasty on me. I'll hold out, don't worry, I won't utter the trigger

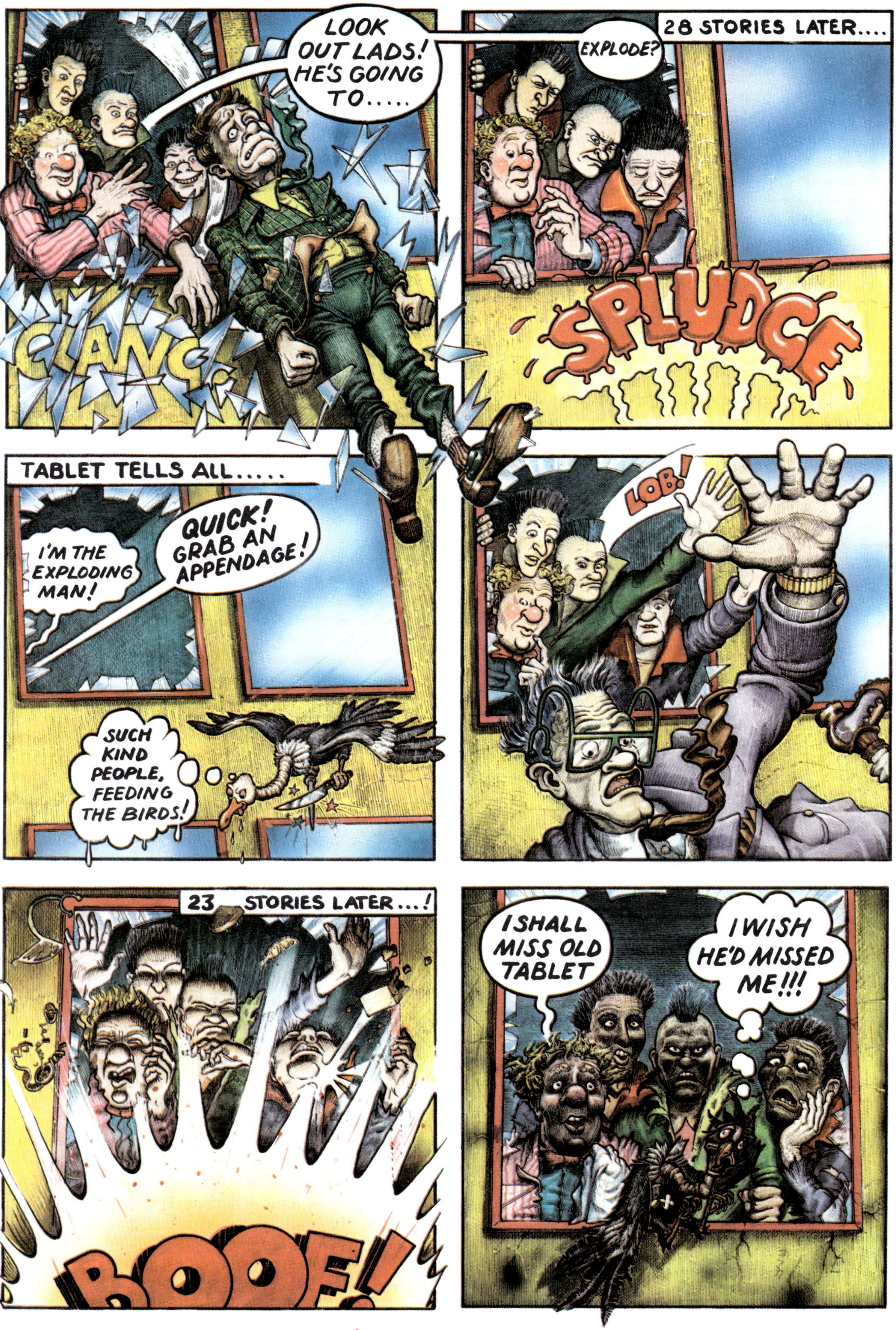

LOOK OUT LADS! HE'S GOING TO.....
CLANG
28 STORIES LATER....
EXPLODE?
SPLUDGE
TABLET TELLS ALL.....
I'M THE EXPLODING MAN!
QUICK! GRAB AN APPENDAGE!
SUCH KIND PEOPLE, FEEDING THE BIRDS!
LOB!

word phrase that will make me explode and blow the Trouser Institute multi-dimensional. Keep a stiff one, I say, keep a stiff one.' Mr Tablet was choking.

'Good kid,' said Trouser, 'Right me jollies, quick, out the window with him, grab an appendage.'

They groped with the dilemmic Tablet, torn between detonation and loyalty, between the glorious Trouser existence and a bloody big bang. Exploding men were going to be the next big phase, for sure. He struggled limply as they heaved him out of the window. Their eyes followed his progress, down, down, and then, bang. He exploded at the fifth floor.

Trouser pulled out a circular curler comb and frothed his golden ringlets around for a while, deep in thought. The two Large Squad, One'ser and Two'ser, were drinking from silver flasks in their purple banana suits. Twiggott was gently humming 'Epitaph' by King Crimson. Their first album was the only good thing they ever did, he was thinking, must have been weird in those days.

'I'm a'glad we's goin' boss', said Twiggott. 'Not worth a wombat's fart dis world ain't.'

The very air seemed charged with speedy silence; the four stood in the hall.

'I jus' 'ope I runs inta Jerry Can and that orange-haired mindboggler, Toni the Cortina. I wanna make sure dey don't collect on da spoils of dis little explodin' phase, know wot I mean, boss?'

'Don't even consider those fish, Twigg, there's no time. No time.'

Chapter 11
Brushing with the Branch Heads

July 27th 2073, Tint Street, Trouser House.

The tunnel of Tint Street had been rolled open to let in the brilliant early morning sunshine and pure blue sky. All that could be heard was the occasional faint whirring of bubble chairs and sometimes a silver saucerette flashed across the blue sky.

Trouser was anxious to get away with as little fuss as possible, so no special arrangements had been made. Trouser House would be taken care of as usual by the reliable Trouser assistants and, on this wonderful morning, the party would slip away on bubble chairs to the London Skyport, and board a saucerette for Almost India.

They arrived strangely close together.

Trouser was standing outside his back door eagerly receiving them. He was wearing Swiss Alpine clothes. Thick braces held his heavy leather shorts up to hang just above the knees, below the shorts were grey socks and big brown boots. On his head (his hair had lost its curls and was smarmed down flat) was a four-sided mountaineer's hat and he carried a flugelhorn. He looked a fool.

'Yipoo yipoo,' he greeted them. 'Like the disguise? An everyday tourist the like of which you see in London every day. Gee honey, ah . . . have you seen our little son, Wilbur? Say Beebee, I think we've lost our little son honey, have you'll seen the little dirt dauber anywheres? Landsakes! Maybe we left him in Switzerland. Now, no no, don't clap, it's a bad habit. Look, I want you to remember; that's my line if we get rumbled, okay? I'm an average tourist with average stupidity.' With that he pulled out a large black sausage and chewed a piece off. 'There. That completes the physical detour; any questions?'

Rodney Shook was On Holiday and said, 'Heeyy Baabiee, like man, where we's goin'? We's goin' to de secret country, bossman?' He swivelled his big white rock 'n' roll eyes.

'Further,' said Trouser, with a strange look in his eye.

The party walked leisurely away from Tint Street and boarded bubble chairs. It was warm even that early, the climate had long since changed, making England one of the warmest countries in the world.

Dil and Dolse had turned up in fine fettle. They were dressed in silver submarine suits which clung tight to their bodies, the suits had black stripes down the side which matched their hair. A lot of the time they were singing, 'Do be do doon doop doop pe do, da do lang lang, da, do lang, lang.' They were now the Biro Sisters, Rodney Shook's back-up chorus. They didn't know what the hell was happening half the time.

Bruce had a hangover from the ball party, not being used to so much coloured wine. He kept on asking Twiggott for some simulated amphetamine

Vaco Pods like this: 'Eh you, you with the green mushroom on yer 'ead, 'ave you got any of them fast pills? I want the old fast pills, I can rob a bank when I'm on them.'

Twiggott was dry with the sealman. 'Take the piss outa my 'at again, wombie, an' I'll force S.T.P. down yer throat an' I'll sit an' look at yer fer a year, understand?'

He didn't.

Mr Straightly had developed a nasty cough by the time they reached the skyport, his moustache drooped sadly and he was sure he was picking up agoraphobia. It was a scourge at that time of the year in London, spread like wildfire.

The clean skyport was just getting lively by 9 o'clock, flights to all parts of the world were coming into operation. What with the winter 'Snow and Ice Orgies' being all the rage, everyone was zooming off to the U.S.A. which was more frozen than unfrozen in the summer months.

The Trouser party, disguised as a group of dumb tourists, were just entering the main skyport doors when they were rudely accosted by a bunch of men with pseudo moose horns on their heads. One of them looked at the glazed Mr Bizarre and told him he ought to go stick his fingers in a glow glob socket and recharge.

Twiggott was in like a shot. 'If you wanna get busted, wombie, youse come to da right place,' he stamped a boot loudly on the artificial marble floor just inside the door. A few people hurried past fearing trouble, for these were the Branch Heads. Renegade anti-Trouser and staunch senility supporters. Their main aim was to bring back fascism and hanging. They were Tedderist, to quote but one of their foul pseudonyms.

The leader was thinking of charging Twiggott with his multi-coloured horns when Trouser went into his detour routine. 'Gee honey, ah . . . have you seen our little son, Wilbur? Say, Beebee, I . . . think we've lost our little son, honey, have ya'll seen the little dirt dauber anywheres? Landsakes, may be we left him in Switzerland!' He pitched his voice rather too high and almost gave the game away; he chewed the black sausage.

'Oo are you?' asked the Branch Heads.

'I told ya, if ya wants to get busted, I'll put a mock astro boot in yer 'ead. Now sponk off!'

Twiggott had put the wind up them. They decided he was a bit on the hasty side and more dangerous than he first appeared so off they stalked, shouting foul slogans. But at least they hadn't recognized Trouser, which was proof of the man's ingenuity in the disguise area.

'Close one there, Twiggott,' whispered Trouser. 'Those Branch Heads are real animal duplicators, of that there's no doubt.'

'Aw boss, no worry there. A quick crack in the standard pills wiv me mock astro's 'ud scare 'em off eggish!'

The fun had started. Everywhere that Trouser went, confusion was sure to follow. They boarded the saucerette for Almost India, the only problem being Bruce and Mr Straightly arguing over who should look after the tickets. In the

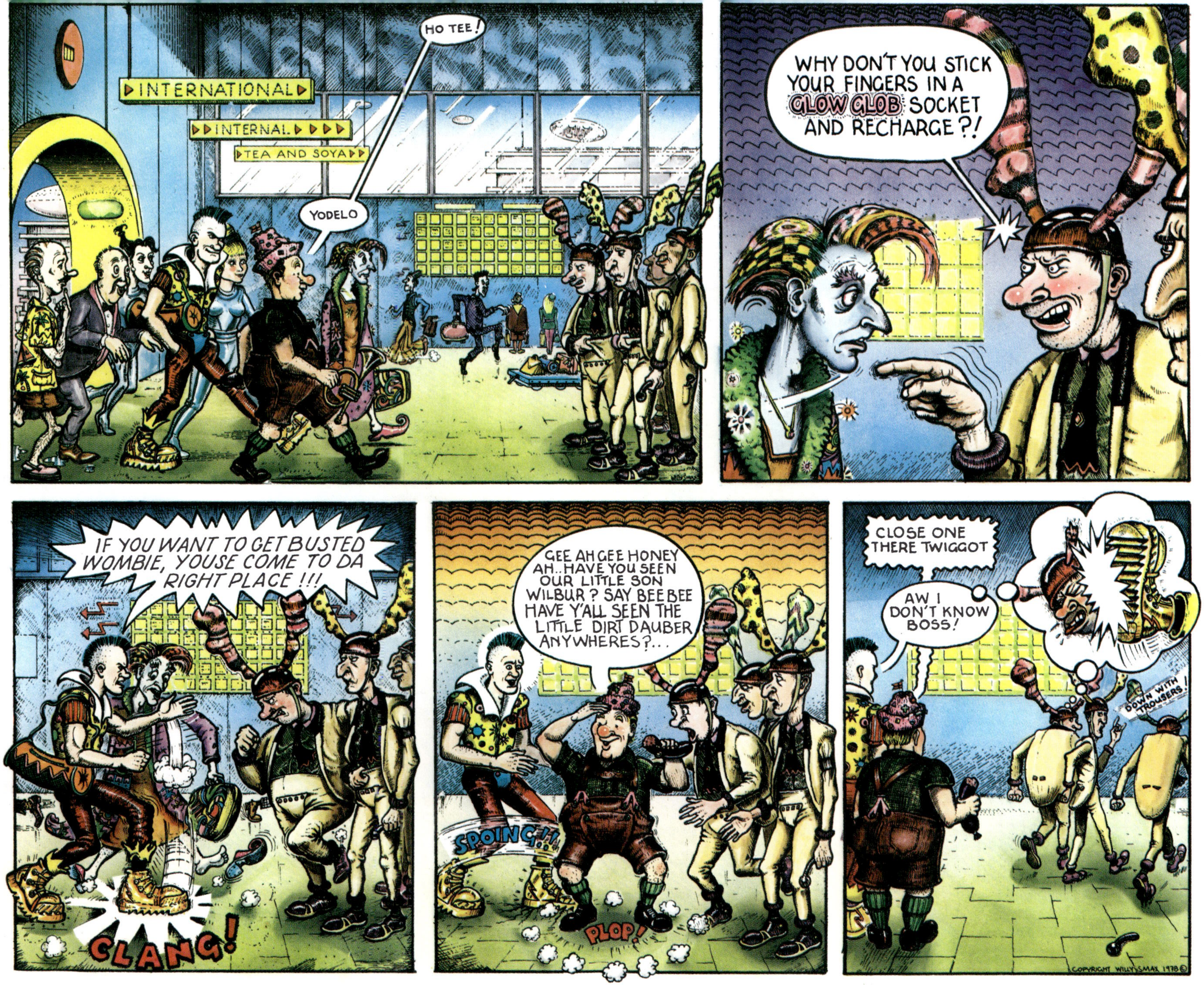

INTERNATIONAL
INTERNAL
TEA AND SOYA
HO TEE!
YODELO

WHY DON'T YOU STICK YOUR FINGERS IN A GLOW GLOB SOCKET AND RECHARGE ?!

end Mr Bizarre put them in his special travelling dander bag, a rare work of subtle design and ideal for tickets, although he usually kept dozens of spare pipes for his smoking mixture in there. It was 9.30 am as the great saucerette lifted gracefully into the blue sky. The hold was stocked mainly with supplies Trouser had had loaded on the night before. A big extended Range Rover was one important item and also a telescopic, collapsible rubber boat, large enough to hold all the Trouser party easily.

The saucerette trip was largely uneventful. Rodney Shook and the Biro Sisters were jamming with two Bob Dylan impersonators, going to Almost India for some almost insight no doubt. They all spoke in drawls and made obvious statements sound profound. Clever bastards, thought the amazing T.G. Trouser who was acting the buffoon but carefully taking everything in.

Bruce was deep in conversation with pubic collector and tight Scotsman, Duffy Wigman. Bruce had a lot to ask him this morning, especially after he'd conned some fast pills from One'ser. 'I say, sporran-knees, do you know anything about Russia? I only ask 'cos I had some muckers from Yorkshire used to hang out in the old sea around there. Is it true it's sunk, is it true what they say, that Russia's a gigantic bomb scare now, eh?'

Duffy looked at the sealman with a concerned expression on his ruddy, whisky soaked face, placing a hand on his nobbly knee just below the sporran. 'Aye, ye might say that Brucey, you're not such a dumb chappie as I had first expected ye know. Russia . . . aye . . . it's a wee bit on the strong side what happened there. Ye see Brucey, there was a wee mangy President of the USA once upon a time, och, way back, way back . . . oooh musta been nineteen-o-blob when they discovered the wee crook had been afiddlin' the books like. Aye . . . unspeakable, I know. Weel, what happened, there was a wee little bit of talk about impeachment or some such, ye know?'

'Not really, chuck,' said Bruce with a maniacal grin. 'Does that mean they threw peaches and assorted fruit at 'im? I'd like to 'ave been there.'

'Nae, ya daft limbo creature yoo! Don't talk like a pankin' woman, man! Roughly speakin', it's a wee canny way o' chucking the bastard out, got me? Aye, but they couldn't pull it off wi' Adrachi Outhouse Innox, a reeght official murderer he was. A real legal crook that man. Anyway, he got away wi' it for the first time, aye, but when they finally discovered the secret electric-chairing o' certain important revolutionaries who had kinda disappeared jus' lately, weel . . . that was the last straw. BUT!' At this point, Duffy Wigman's eyes were gleaming rather hysterically and he was leaning very close to Bruce, his attentive listener. 'What happened jus' then was a reel turn-up, one hour after they stormed the White House to drag the bastard oot by his head, he ordered for the perilous button ta be pressed, aye. Ye ken what that means, Brucey boy? I'll tell ye what it means. It means a great fleet of dirty great atomic bombs went hurling off to the poor unsuspecting Soviet Union and blew the place to wee single pieces! Not a shred of the Fatherland left, blown to porridge! Dastardly.'

Bruce was intrigued.

The party was in the lounge now, chatting loosely, keeping a lookout for trouble. It was Twiggott who spotted it first, as usual. Mr Straightly was idly chatting away to two suspicious looking characters leaning against the bar. Twiggott noticed that the excitable Mr Straightly was telling the strangers of the knee and fez incident at Trouser's party. The Great Trouser protector extraordinary was anxious that the game wasn't given away in idle conversation, so he approached the three at the bar.

One of the men was dressed like a fountain pen, the other looked like a big shiny gum-boot. Both had heavy make-up on their faces and and big green moustaches. Twiggott looned up behind the bubbling Mr Straightly and tapped him on the shoulder.

'Oh, I say, top-hole Twiggott, old can, just conversing with these two upright citizens over here, nothing untoward, I assure you, sir.' He grinned nervously under the cool eye of Twiggott.

'Well, das awright, but jus' keep it cool and standard, see? Don't collect any 'angers-on like eh, 'cos ya know we ain't got room, bein' an average tourist party wiv a strict timetable, understand?'

'Of course, Twiggott, sir, you know me, discretion as in brolly stand, what!'

The two figures leaning against the clear plastic bar drank soya beer delicately. The one with the fountain pen disguise spoke in a stilted foreign sounding accent, he sounded as if he was talking with a grill between his teeth. 'Is zis flight goingk to take very long could you tell me? Haf ve left the ground yet? I hear tha vishing is good in Almost India.'

Twiggott looked closely at the speaker, he couldn't see his mouth because it was covered with the bottom of his pen nib hat. There was something about him, thought Twiggott, something smelly. 'Naw to da first, yes to da second, and der ain't any fish in Almost India to da third. Does dat answer yer question, Mr Fountain?'

'Zer name is Pincer, Mr Pincer.'

They shook hands tentatively. Mr Pincer's friend, dressed as a gum-boot, said nothing. Twiggott thought he could see his hand shaking under that shiny plastic.

'Vell, better ve get goingk before zer rain comes, ze you zoon.'

They turned and walked away from the bar across the brilliant purple carpet to the corridor. But as they did, from the back of the pen nib, dropped a few strands of orange hair. Twiggott watched it hang limply for a while until he suddenly grew sure he recognised that shade of orange and that walk; it must be his arch irritator and organ surgeon, Toni the Cortina! Of course it was and Twiggott, in his surprise, shouted 'Oy!' They turned around for a brief instant and then bolted off down the corridor. Twiggott was just about to give chase when Trouser rushed over and stopped him.

'No Twigg! Leave it. Leave it be: I suspected Jerry Can and Toni the Cortina were in here somewhere from the first, but if we start ripping the ship up searching for them, the game will be up. And I'm not talking about the head game, savvy?'

'Sponk it,' hissed Twiggott through his teeth as he glared after the already vanished renegades. 'I wanna know 'ow. I wanna git to da bottom of dis and some soft centre is gonna get purchased.' He was angry, but Trouser knew how to handle him; he passed him a Holiday Pod and sat down and chatted to him, explaining that the party only had to keep its collective wits together and no one could stop it. They must continue as planned at all costs; if anyone found out the truth of their mission, it would probably be the last chance. Trouser seemed more concerned with the sudden transformation of Mr Tablet, who was once a debonair Music Therapist with a good eye for diagnosis and then suddenly was ready to explode and blow his old colleagies and most of Central M.T. into the other side.

He got Twiggott involved in trying to figure how it was done and they were deep in conversation when a nasty shout broke the quiet chatter of the saucerette lounge. The travellers sitting in the lounge, the Trouser party and about ten other people, looked around and saw two Bob Dylan impersonators engaged in a heavy argument.

'Naw look, if's you sing "Mr Tambourine Man" again, I'll contact ma superiors and git you sued,' said one of them, pointing an accusing finger at the other.

'Well that does it,' retaliated the other, 'that just about does it. How can you be Bob Dylan man? Huh? Answer me that! Bob Dylan wouldn't talk that kinda bullshit, I'm gonna take that title man, 'cos I don't talk bullshit.'

'You . . . what . . . Jesus! Look man, you sing another line of that song an' I'll twist your ear, naw, I wrote that song only last night on ma little typewriter and you musta overhead me asingin' it to Joanie and filched it, man.'

'You're crazy! I wrote "Mr Tambourine Man" a week ago and I got a record to prove it, buddy. Besides you ain't even got a guitar!'

Mr Bizarre hated the sight of blood, it always made him start reciting poetry to cleanse the air, so he decided to step in. He lurched forward, bird-like

SSHH!
LISTEN! I WROTE MR. TAMBOURINE MAN!!
YOU FILCHED IT MAN!
©WILLYSMAX 1979

SING IT AGAIN AND I'LL TWIST YOUR EAR!!!
£76 IN THIS STYLE
HUH! YOU GOT A LOT O' NERVE!

COOL THE BUD BOYS, USE THE VIBRO SPACER..

ARE YOU GONNA VIBE THIS OUT BUDDY?
NO! I'M THE REAL DYLAN!

THEN THERE'S ONLY ONE COURSE OF ACTION LEFT..

RIGHT!
BARMAN! WE GO TO VIOLENCE ISLAND!!

in his turned-up-toe mandarin shoes and artist's apron, complete with paint. He pulled out a little Holiday-Plus gun, a sort of handbag Music Therapy device designed by the Great Trouser for emergencies, and he offered it to the boys in denim.

'Cool the bud, cool the bud, bind the splinters with mental horse hair and vanquish foul dust stirred unbeknowing of the rubber tubed one.'

'Do you vibe this out, buddy, or are you still insistin' you wrote that song?'

It was getting hard to tell one from the other now.

'No chance, kid, no chance. I'm the real Bob Dylan, take it or leave it, but if you're gonna leave it, you know what that means?'

'Yeah, an' I'm sure gonna leave it!'

'Right, then we settle this in the only way we know how; we go to Violence Island.'

The words made Mr Bizarre shudder and so he tripped back to his seat and carried on flicking nutron pills down his red throat. The public service of Violence Island would now be thrust immediately into action.

That was the last thing Trouser wanted. He shrugged his shoulders and chewed moodily on a piece of the black sausage. It meant a delay of twenty-four hours while the saucerette changed course for Violence Island and refuelling had to take place.

Chapter 12
Violence Island

'Christ! This whole affair is most untrouserous, most untrouserous,' said the man himself.

'Yes, dashed uncouth, Mr Trouser, sir, I wonder . . . is this mission worth continuing with?'

They were sitting in a wooden shack while the saucerette refuelled. Outside you could hear the occasional scream or obscene phrase as people fought it out. Mr Trouser bobbed over to the window and looked out at the rocky terrain. The sky was blue and it was quiet and still out there in the heat. A lonely figure dressed as a soldier dashed out from behind a rock and vanished again. Trouser watched with boredom. Then he shook his pink cheeks and sniffed through his dumpy nose as he turned round to face Mr Straightly who was sitting on a wooden bench, drinking tea from a big white mug. 'You know, sometimes I wonder about you, Mr Straightly. Is this mission worth continuing, indeed,' He sounded a little scornful.

'Well I . . . I only tho . . .'

'You only tho . . .' said Mr Trouser.

'I only tho . . .' said Mr Straightly.

'You only tho . . .' said Trouser.

They went on like this for some minutes; they got stuck on the word 'thought', it was an amazing spectacle that didn't happen too often but was definitely on the increase. Bruce thought it was great fun and rolled up laughing, his whiskers were bright pink this morning. Outside Twiggott heard the commotion and strode in, cursing Bruce and interfering in the trapped conversation to break the sequence.

'You two awright,eh?'

'Yes, yes, thank you, Twigg, old sugar plum,' said Trouser with a smile and a hop.

Poor Mr Straightly had put his arms out limply in front of him, as if groping in the dark; he looked extremely baffled.

Trouser handed him a little yellow pill with a face on it. 'Now now, old horse, don't confuse the pineapple, here take this and put on a new face.'

Outside the two Bob Dylan impersonators were kicking hell out of each other. They were soon joined by two old and battered ex-Sergeant Majors who took sides and gave strategic advice. They were Sergeant Major Paragonk and Sergeant Major Surplus, two men who had decided to stay on Violence Island, having scorned Music Therapy and Holiday Pods for a valiant life of rampage and rape.

The island itself was in the middle of the Indian Ocean and was a necessary part of the great escape from the out and out cut and thrust of society.

If you had enough reason and decided you didn't want to soothe out the nasties with Music Therapy, Violence Island was the place to get it out of your system. You could batter people in a like state to yourself without dragging bystanders in. It was the only solution. There were no weapons other than stones and clubs and anything else you could scrape out of the barren landscape. It was at first thought that the inhabitants of Violence Island might possibly get themselves together and storm the nearest mainland: fortunately, this had never happened. After a good punch-up people generally went back refreshed and the best of friends although some went a little too far. But of course, murder was legal on the island, you took your chances.

The two Bob Dylan impersonators were throwing sods of earth at each other under the supervision of the two totally mad Sergeant Majors. The Biro Sisters leant against the dividing fence and watched the fun. It was a good day for spectators as a dozen or so people had formed gangs and were having a full-scale war. A bloody arm came flying over a little hillock a few hundred yards from the fence; it wiggled for a while.

Otherwise, it was a boring night the party spent and there was no sign of the dastardly Trouser opposition, which only served to make Twiggott and the Large Squad more and more aggravated: they were beginning to think that this hold-up had been planned so that an attempt on Trouser's life could be made. They were right, it was a fiendish conspiracy and, by midnight, the Trouser party, who were reclining in the saucerette lounge, were starting to sense the tension.

Without warning, bursting through the swing doors, came Jerry Can and Toni the Cortina and the doors at the other end of the lounge leading to the entertainments room swung open to reveal the Round Lads.

Rodney Shook screamed 'Mercy!' and the Biro Sisters stopped 'do doing'. The Large Squad were nowhere to be seen, they had been out in the shack watching floodlight Violence through the window when they were coshed, tied, and gagged by the Round Lads.

'Welcome to Violence Island, fat Trouser. I trust you're not enjoying your stay,' said Toni the Cortina with a smug bow. He was dressed in a purple jump suit with tweed boots, in his hand he held a coiled-up whip of blue leather. Jerry Can wore an orange pullover and jet heavy jeans, in his hand was a nasty looking cast iron shilelagh. A black cigarette hung from his lips. As they stepped into the lounge, they were followed by the two Bob Dylan impersonators, armed with bricks and pieces of wood. It looked a bit tricky for Trouser.

'Well, ahem. So nice of you to drop in, you crooked pair of wombies, what a tasteful get-up Toni, can't say your hack surgeon friend has changed much though, still looks a scruff.' Trouser was taking chances here, but he had faith in destiny and could not believe in an untimely death although capture seemed imminent and possible torture likely.

'Tell me, you ugly sponkers, how did you manage this? All a little ruse I do hope, you're surely not serious with all this Trouser opposition, I mean I'm just a replica you know, just an automaton, look, national health teeth.' He smiled and showed them his teeth. They weren't falling for it though.

The Cortina spoke. 'If you want to know the details, Trouser, the two Bob Dylan impersonators here are a couple of old buddies looking for action and the Round Lads landed on the Island yesterday pissed out of their crusts, pretending they had a grudge to settle. Let's face it, Trous, you've been stormed. So why not – and I am addressing YOU TOO, TWIGGOTT!' He glared at Twiggott who was polishing his gold boot. 'Why not come quietly, eh?'

'Where's me henchies then eh, where are they, that's wot I wanna know, where's da Large Squad?' demanded Twiggott.

'Taken care of they are for sure,' said Jerry Can with a real death and destruction feel to his voice.

'Take 'em!' shouted Toni the Cortina. Out cracked his whip. It caught poor Mr Straightly right in the left ear and stung like hell but surprisingly the man's courage grew and grew and at the thought of this awful intimidation.

'You bounders! You scourge of the land. Keep the old school walking, I say, top hole and butcher the bandits!' And up he leapt to deliver Toni the Cortina a hefty naked knee in the groin. He danced back with surprising agility only to bump his head on the back of Bruce's, and out he went like a light.

'Ee by 'eck, you daft bugger,' said Bruce, rubbing his head and staggering around. The Round Lads were ponderous compared to Twiggott's henchies and, as they rushed Trouser, Mr Bizarre shot a herd of miniature sticky camels at them from his infinity box, he was a good one for supplying the confusion; they didn't know what to make of this at all. You just can't bash people about with a plastic sticky camel stuck to your cheek. In came Twiggott like a fighting machine, cracking a Round Lad in the face with his left mock astro, pirouetting and repeating the action several times. But they were outnumbered, for Bruce had been coshed by Jerry Can's cast iron shilelagh and was out for the count, and Rodney Shook was clean out of Mad-Rubber and didn't feel in the mood for this sort of thing. Trouser had only a half portion of black sausage for a weapon and was soon struggling under the grip of his arch enemies. Things looked ill, but where was the dubious pornographic Scotsman, Duffy Wigman?

The fighting got more strenuous and Twiggott was feeling the strain, his arm was bleeding badly. His beautiful zebra suit was ripped a bit, that annoyed him the most. Mr Trouser was in the grip of Toni the Cortina and Jerry Can.

It was, of course, Duffy Wigman who saved the day. He had inadvertently wandered over the barrier and onto the battlefield, finding himself mixed up in some nasty situations. When he found his way back to the waiting room, he discovered the Large Squad all tied up with their shocked hair sticking up skywards. Being a fellow of quick wit, he untied them and organized a plan of attack. In his own words, they would 'Rush the culprits and mangle their wee heads.'

Just as Trouser had been chloroformed and Twiggott was on his last fighting breath, in they came, looking like a herd of golliwogs. The element of surprise scared the Bob Dylan impersonators out of their minds and they were gone in a flash. There was much bashing and rolling but soon the big, ugly and somewhat drably attired Round Lads were scattered all over the lounge. Twiggott blocked the door so that Jerry Can and Toni the Cortina were forced to give in. It was another victory for Music Therapy.

STOMP!
WILLY SMAX COPYRIGHT © 1979

Chapter 13
The Boloovial Fish

'It's all ill wind that makes the room smell, Twiggott, wouldn't you agree?' said T.G. Trouser, in a tatty white robe and weather-stained raincoat. He addressed Twiggott, dabbing antiseptic onto his swollen eye.

'Yeah, sure,' groaned Twiggott. 'I still fink we shoulda dumped J.C. and Co. inta the middle of da big wet one, boss, they'll only cause more irrit wherever dey is, bastards.' Twiggott leaned back in the bubble seat and painfully drank soya beer. 'Me ribs 'urt a bit,' he said.

'No, no, no,' continued Trouser. 'Never shall I hold a grudge against those half-cast pornbrokers, Twigg. So bad for the Karma, grudges, so bad. We needed reminding of the opposition, it's cleared the air.'

Trouser's tiny blue eyes looked thinly on Bruce who was operating the rat-splatter. He shook his jowl a little and rubbed a hand over his flat blond hair. In the scuffle his nose had been hit, it was now very swollen and red and looked just like a false one.

The saucerette was in the air and about to reach Almost India, and the Trouser party were, by and large, still intact. They had left those treacherous rogues on Violence Island under the guidance of the totally mad Sergeant Majors. Duffy Wigman had told the Sergeant Majors that they had come to the island to beat each other to blazes. That would keep them occupied for a while at least.

Trouser was watching the Range Rover emerge from the hold of the saucerette in the skyport at Almost India. 'I do hope she's as good as the adverts, Bizer,' he said.

'I can't stipulate that, can I?' said Bizer not really hearing what Trouser said as he puffed very loudly on his smoking mixture.

With very little trouble the group were on their way, towing a trailer with many supplies both outrageous and largely unnecessary. Mr Straightly had brought along his moose head, Duffy Wigman had packed three hundredweight of strawberry flavoured artificial porridge – a stickler for tradition that one – Dil and Dolse, the Biro Sisters, had their double sleeping bag with portholes. Mr Bizarre had vaious gadgets and a hundredweight of carfully prepared smoking mixture, and the incredible Rodney Shook had packed a variety of different instruments, all hand made. Twiggott and the Large Squad had a few clubs and things, just in case. And Trouser, growing attached to the animal, had packed the cow, 'Three Points to the Home Team', complete with moos, into a big wooden box.

They made good time and soon reached the Nepalese border after driving through the night, speeded up on blue coded Holiday Pods. Rodney Shook wrote ten songs and the Biro Sisters admitted they were in love. They celebrated by buying a few gallons of the local Bonkers Juice in a Nepalese Government shop.

As they drove along the dirt track, passing imitation beggars and other riffraff, Mr Straightly turned very, very pale, right down to his English knees.

'Gad, I'm having a most remarkable déjà vu experience, it's incredible, bally confusing.'

They all told him to shut up and he almost had a nasty turn when he realized he had actually been here before, on that fateful night when the gallant Trouser came struggling across the wastes in the very same guise he wore now. It was all too much for the khaki-shorted Mr Straightly.

It was broad daylight this time, and Trouser, sitting in the front passenger seat chewing the top of a hair dye bottle, was leaning out of the window staring intently at the landscape. Twiggott was at the wheel, dressed in a cute two-piece 'map of the world' T-shirt suit. Trouser leaned over and studied his back for directions.

'The rain in Spain falls mainly on the peasants and, by my calculations, we should be quite near the secret entrance to Javaal, ah ha, ah ha, STOP!'

Twiggott brought the vehicle to a lurching halt and out jumped Trouser himself right into a pothole that unfortunately was deeper than it looked. He was up to his neck in muddy water. After they dragged him out soaking and flushed, he said, 'Well could be worse, might have been the trusty body box.' They admired his cool. 'Now, see that bunch of flora growing in a loose rough-hinged manner over there?' he pointed to the thick scrub on the border line.

'Yes,' they all said together.

'Well, it's got nothing to do with us at all, not at all, ignore it completely, it's of no consequence.'

They all cheered the electric Jesus.

'What we're after is a formation of rocks, boulders, and other debris typical of rugged underprivileged areas such as this, THERE!' he bellowed and gesticulated enjoying his 'I'm a clever bugger and know where we are performance'. Back they jumped into the Range Rover and approached the collection of rocks which loomed up on the side of the track blocking out the sun. 'Right Twiggott,' said the man. 'I want you to drive straight for that big brick, there.' He pointed a tubby finger at the flat side of the rock face. Twiggott aimed the vehicle towards it and then suddenly realized what he was asked to do and jammed on the trusty disc brakes. He stared at Trouser for a while, 'What goes on, boss? Am I ta believe you wants me ta do the ole suicidal on da mission?'

'Twiggott, old son. Have trust in the Trouser, drive straight for that looming text book sheer rock face.'

'But, boss, we's gonna prang like a suburb trendy on a Sunday afternoon, I can't do dat!'

'Twiggott,' said Trouser with slow deliberation, looking fatherly into Twiggot's eyes.

'Yeah,' said Twiggott miserably.

'Do you know the story of the lonely chap in the green sports car who

DRIVE FOR THAT SHEER TEXT BOOK ROCK FACE TWIGGOT!!
GULP
FORWARD TO VICTORY!!
HERE WEGOES THEN!
TO JAVAAL!
FLYT 505JT
VAROOOOOM!
CRUMP!
DRRUM!

couldn't find a female frontispiece cardboard pre-conditioned normality in a microcosm, to sit in his passenger seat and accompany him to the dire post cloth cap illusion? So he used to drive around with a tree in his car. Damn great rhododendron?' Trouser looked serious at least.

'Well no, I've never 'eard dat one, boss,' said Twiggott.

'Right, it just goes to show you've got a lot to pick up yet, my lad, a damn lot. Forward in first gear and to victory.' From the back somewhere came a sneaky giggle from Bruce.

'Hah . . . alright den, here we goes,' sighed the doubting driver.

The Range Rover plunged for the rock and, on impact, the genius Trouser shouted loudly, 'To Javaal!' Rodney Shook screamed 'Mercy,' and the Range Rover collided with a fearful smack just as everyone except Trouser expected it to do. Large pieces of chrome and chips of paint fell off, it made a nasty dent in the front.

'Well, Christ, what da pank do you expect, Trous. I mean, issa sponkin' great rock innit?'

Trouser leapt out and inspected first the rock, and then the damage, shaking his head in disbelief. 'Ahum, well, we all make them, Senor, oui oui, sacre pink, sacre pink.' It was rather an anticlimax. He trundled off down the track until he came to a similar rock face which he prodded for a while with a piece of mangled chrome. The others got out to drink some Bonkers Juice and stretch their legs.

'This seems to respond,' shouted Trouser, 'point it at this one, this is it, no doubt.'

Bruce whispered to Mr Bizarre and Duffy Wigman as they climbed back in, 'Hee eee, I think ee's blown a corpuscle, eee . . . daft bugger's a berk with an 'e', understand, chuck?' They didn't, but got the general impression.

'Who else shall we follow in these dark times?' asked Duffy Wigman, quietly gritting his yellow teeth and opening a whisky bottle the hard way.

'Awright, if you wanna wreck dis body box, I don't mind, boss, gives me a dirty great adrenalin flash, dis does. It's getting back to civilization I'm worried about. It's a longish walk from 'ere for tired wombies in da midday sun.'

'Forward in first!' said Trouser staring ahead defiantly.

'Sure ya don't want me ta reverse into it dis time and do da back in?'

Trouser didn't answer, but started humming 'Land of Hope and Glory'.

Twiggott did as he was told and this time the rock face responded in the way Trouser had expected. Instead of another nasty crash, the party were plunged into darkness. Trouser flicked a switch and on came the headlights to reveal the dry walls of a cave, just large enough for the Range Rover to pass through. Twiggott stopped and twisted around to look through the back window but could only see thick darkness. He chewed his lip for a while, staring at Trouser.

'Awright, wod 'appened?'

'I can answer that one sitting down, if it's alright by everyone?' No one seemed to object to Trouser's request. 'You see, although it appeared to be a solid slab of granite, what we have just plundered through is merely a disguise.

The entrance to the secret country is a girt flap of surplus formica which closes again after impact, you can't even see the join. Forward.'

They drove on through the dark cave for what seemed like hours until suddenly without warning the Range Rover was bumping through thick undergrowth where the sun could barely glint. Mr Straightly was deeply disturbed, and Twiggott cursed as he steered between the knobbly tree roots and mounds of earth. It was just starting to get uncomfortably hot when the foliage thinned out rapidly and they found themselves on a dusty track similar to the one on the other side of the secret entrance. Trouser became more jubilant with every change of scenery and was soon doing plant imitations to keep everyone amused. Bruce had fallen deeply asleep and dreamed, again, of the sea.

Approaching a fork in the track, Trouser signalled to turn left, and soon they were straining their eyes to see what the strip of twinkling silver was in the distance, threading its way across a flat sandy plain. Of course, it was a river, or a canal anyway.

It was man-made out of shiny rectangular bricks and cut a deep triangle into the desert-like plain. Where the track ended the canal began and, on closer inspection, the water was a pea-soup green bordered by orangeish yellow bricks. It looked rather nice and the Trouser expedition relaxed for a while, staring into its smurky green depths where no weed or debris whatsoever obscured the symmetry of the view down the canal, winding to infinity. Bruce was in like a shot.

After a while, the boat was inflated and its flag, which bore the slogan, 'Trouser for Pope,' was erected. Bruce finally emerged, puffing and wheezing.

'Eee bloody 'ell, it's as smooth as a bloody bath-tub down there. Nice, though. 'Ear, is there anything to jump in this Javaal place, eh? Could I . . . like, you know, make a jump there? If there's no crutch there I reckon I'll set up home in this 'ere giant urinal, nice and damp, heh . . .' Bruce spoke with almost fanatical glee.

Trouser walked up to him, smoking a bright yellow cigar, and limply laid an arm over Bruce's shoulder.

'No worries, baby, zooming, man. There's more women in Javaal than brain cells in your grey knot of half-human phlegm, can you dig it, man? Ha ha, anyway, Bruce, surely you could like, make with the changes, eh? C'mon now, whiskers, don't act like a testicle.'

'Are you a bloody queer or something, mate?'

Trouser slipped on a a large pair of purple sunglasses and stared down the canal, moving his head rigidly from side to side, smiling like an American.

Mr Bizarre stared after the Range Rover left standing in the hot sun as the inflatable boat drifted down the still canal. There was no sound save the occasional plop of water as Duffy Wigman and Mr Straightly leisurely rolled the red plastic oars. The boat was black and rubbery like a massive tyre, and it was stacked full with the party's paraphernalia.

Bizer, rising to the occasion, had put on his flying jacket and pilot's cap and strapped his goggles across his forehead. He saluted the Range Rover

'Damn Froggies have got the wind up.' He was confused to say the least.

Mr Straightly was sitting down wiping the sweat from his brow with a yellow and green striped tie when he noticed something in the water. At first he ignored it, thinking it was an hallucination but no, it happened again.

It was definitely something underneath the water, something large and probably alive. Every now and then it rolled just under the surface and created a swirl, following the boat along the canal. He turned about him to see if it was Bruce in there again, but the seal-being was on board, also intently gazing into the deeps.

'I say, Bruce old chap, do you . . . ah . . . do you see what I see, something bally well floundering about down there?'

'I've seen it, Mr Straightly, I don't know what it is, but it's a nifty little mover.' Bruce had a faraway look in his eye, his teeth jutted out like a mountain range and his eyes were glazed. Mr Straightly turned to look into the water again and Bruce was gone, slipping quietly over the side.

Rodney Shook had got to his feet and was ploughing into his latest non-million seller, 'I got to stop goin' before I stop to go'. It was a gem and soon there was much handclapping and finger-snapping going on. 'Rock like a boat, Rodney,' was the tight backing chorus from the Biro Sisters, 'Rock like a boat.'

After some time, Mr Straightly began to feel anxious for his friend, so he called over to T.G. Trouser, who was doing the Stormcock, the latest dance craze. They'd gone quite a considerable distance since Bruce had gone over the side, and there had been no more sign of the mysterious underwater life.

'I say, Mr Trouser, sir, have you got a moment?'

'What? Oh, infinity baby, just dig it,' said Trouser.

It was at times like these that Mr Straightly felt frustrated at the antics of the overweight Trouser, the man just didn't seem to take things seriously, and Mr Straightly was having severe doubts about his decision to leave the Music Therapy empire and rush off on what would probably turn out to be a wild goose chase.

Trouser glanced back in the middle of his dance step and noted the harried expression on Mr Sraightly's patchy face. 'Well, well, what's up then? You look as though you've just grappled with a ghost.'

'Oh, it may be nothing, Mr Trouser, sir, but . . . well, there was something writhing about down there. Something bally big, and I fear Bruce has bung ho'd over the side to investigate.' Mr Straightly was twitching violently as he spoke. He was wishing he'd informed his old Auntie Paperclip before he left Engand.

'He's gone over the side?' asked Trouser.

'Well that's nothing, I expect he's . . .' The words fell away and Trouser's mouth gaped open as he saw the spectacle in the water just behind Mr Straightly's back. Just a few feet behind the stern, Bruce was bobbing up and down in the water. But he was not alone. His left arm was draped around the shoulders of a very large fish.

Its body was grey green, with large shiny scales, and it had a long snout-like face, like that of a porpoise. It was about the same size as Bruce, judging from the size of its shoulders which were pressed closely against the sealman in a friendly manner. Its eyes were big and round and definitely female, with giant black eyelashes and just a hint of mascara. On the end of its snout was a large pair of bright fleshy lips all pursed out and prominent with red lipstick.

'Bruce! Put that brazen hussy back where you found her at once!' It was Mr Bizarre who had spoken and soon the others were watching the scene.

Bruce giggled. 'Don't be bloody daft, Mr Bizarre, She's a real friend this one is, she's a bit lonely too. There's not many like her these days, you know.'

Mr Straightly hiccuped loudly and Duffy Wigman passed him the whisky bottle with a slow grunt.

'D'you want to know what she is? I'll tell you. She's a Boloovial fish.'

'A Boloovial fish?' echoed some of the party.

'S'right, a Boloovial fish. she's on the change, like me, but hasn't really taken to it yet. It's not easy you know, it's all right for you lot.'

The couple bobbed up and down in the water, and her provocative eyes flashed appealingly and shyly at the crowd of onlookers. Bruce looked very sad but at the same time hopeful. It was the look of a man who knows there is little understanding between people and even when he feels he has found the answer, realizes that it is only transient. That it is only relief for a while. Mr Straightly's heart went out to him.

'Yes, cute little bugger, isn't she,' said Bruce looking into her eyes thought fully. 'Boloovial fish, you see, they 'ave trouble breeding. For the Boloovial fish eats itself.'

'Eats itself?' spluttered Duffy Wigman. 'Explain yourself, Brucey, ah canny ken yoor oold fishy tales, can ye noo clarify the matter?'

'I said it eats itself. Not for dinner like, but it just does, it just eats itself. That's why there's so few of 'em left. It's bloody daft, I know, but that's what they do.'

'Well . . . come on now, Bruce, enough of this horticulture, back on board, back to the fold.' It was T.G. Trouser who spoke at last after a pause as everyone stared at the wonderful fish-being.

Bruce looked balefully at the water just under his mouth before he answered. 'Can't,' he said.

'You can't! But I say, old boy, has this . . . this . . . thing put some kind of curse on you?' Mr Straightly spoke rather half-heartedly, and only because he wanted the best for Bruce. 'Don't be so contrary, old sport, we all like you here, damn it all.'

'It's very nice of you, Mr Straightly, I know you're me friend, although I'm not so sure about some of the others,' he glanced at Twiggott swiftly and balefully.

'Aw now don't get soppish on me, kid. Ya knows I'd look after ya. Look, dis ain't any ole dumb excursion, dis is da Trouser dumb excursion! See? An' dat means yer in, Wombie, yer in. An' ya can't get more in dan being in wiv da Trouser. Fool he might be, but friend he always is.' Twiggott stood legs astride with his green hair cut in his hand, gesticulating.

His wide smile almost convinced Bruce to think twice, and the Large

Squad mumbled agreement. Trouser coughed and opened his eyes wide. He wasn't sure he liked the bit about being a fool. It was a funny old world, he thought, one way and another.

Bruce sighed and looked again into the eyes of the Boloovial fish. 'Ahhh . . . no, it's no good, I've got to give it a try. I think I need somethin' to settle me down a bit. I'd only get you all into trouble by robbing a bank or something.'

But they didn't catch his last words. The boat was drifting away from them on some unknown current, and the silent onlookers waved back at Bruce. The Boloovial fish lifted a flipper and waved gently as her eyes gave one last flash down the straight green canal. The dusk brought stars and memories of childhood. It was time to sleep.

Chapter 14
Kurly Krishna the Kellogg Kid

'Okay, you slugs, come and get it!' said T.G. Trouser, bashing pans together as everyone stirred in the already hot morning sun. The boat had come a long way during the night and above the high steep banks grew thick jungle vegetation and the clamour of parrots could be heard shrill across the air.

'Oh I say . . . this is a trifle foolish,' said Mr Straightly, yawning, stretching and looking around. 'We've surely made a miscalculation and landed in the bally tropics. By thunder, there may be tigers about!' Mr Straightly grew excited at the thought and quickly searched for his white hunter's hat and clean white shorts.

'Tigers. Tygers. Tiegerz.' repeated Mr Bizarre betwen Vegipills.

'Which doth remind myself,' said Trouser snapping his fingers silently. "Three Points to the Home Team" needs a clump of trusty fodder be now.' He got Twiggott to open the big box and give the cow a plate of pills.

Everyone turned rapidly when Dolse, of the Biro Sisters, gave a loud shrill scream. 'Ahhh! Look, a snake!' she shouted. Creeping over the side of the boat was indeed, a fat, long, polka-dot snake. Its head lolled from side to side and its forked tongue hissed in and out, aimed towards Dolse's crutch. She sat terrifed and prostrate as the thing moved nearer.

'Don't blow a corpuscle! There's no need to fear, it's just a robot.' T.G. Trouser spoke with confidence as he sneaked up on the snake which had pulled itself completely on board.

'Aye, weel, we dinne want a natural history lesson, Trouser. Reeght now that wee bastard could be dangerous, who cares what bloody species it is.' It was Duffy who snapped impatiently.

'Don't be such a wee highland fling, Duffy Wigman!' warned Trouser. 'I said it's a robot, you know? Circuits, wires, etc? Computer programmers with false moustaches? Lab technicians with haemorrhages? Understand?'

Mr Bizarre almost did.

'Now, if I can just arrest its writhings . . . the situation will be entirely under controohoh ohch!!' Trouser had misjudged and, after creeping up stealthily, he now found himself with the snake's mouth clamped around his hand. 'Sponk! Bloody nuisance these things; no, it's alright, it's jaws are only stainless steel, no fangs, none at all. I'll just crack it across the cap of your boot, One'ser.'

One'ser thrust his mock astro outwards and Trouser smacked the snake across the black toe-cap with expert precision. Six inches of the snake stayed fiercely on his tubby hand, the rest, about 20 feet, dropped over the side and sank, writhing to the bottom.

Trouser shook and shook but could not budge the mouth open. 'Tch tch.

They're becoming a scourge in these parts, false reptiles. All over the bloody show. LOOK OUT! there's an automated spider monkey!'

The tiny robot monkey came swinging across the canal on a thick green vine. It dipped a spindly hand and snatched startled Two'ser's black pork-pie hat. 'Jesus, gettin' a bit nasty init? Shall we get the clubs out, Twigg?' he said.

Twiggott was considering arms when Trouser stepped in. 'Don't bother, boy, they're quite harmless. A little aggroid mayhap, but quite harmless. Any rate, we're nearing our destination soon, got to keep a lookout for our guide. Tiny little bugger, you could miss him if he stood sideways. Hell of a head though, zombied into yesterday.'

The green canal seemed to be shrinking in size, or perhaps it was the dense jungle growth, no one could be sure. Trouser was straining his eyes into the thick greenery for signs of life. He was doing his best to ignore the six inches of snake hanging from his wrist. 'Easy on the paddle, can't be long now,' he said.

Duffy Wigman slugged on the whisky and dropped the empty bottle over the side, collecting, as he did so, a slightly annoyed look from Trouser and a faint 'Tch tch.' The miniscule but rugged Scotsman then pulled up his kilt and started pissing into the water.

Mr Straightly was On Holiday and staring heavily into the luxuriant tropical growth. He lost his way deep inside a large pink flower and suddenly became intensely poetic. 'Golly,' he sighed, 'It's all a bit like something straight out of a fairy tale.'

Duffy Wigman burped loudly and said, 'Hah, nay man, it's straight outa ma groin.'

'Hey boss, is it my imagination just doing its stuff, or is that a little man?' It was Rodney Shook, who had put down his harmonica to speak. He had, in fact, seen their guide and host, founder of the new non-religion 'Spannerism' and Cosmic Clown inferior, Kurly Krishna the Kellogg Kid.

He stood, or rather half-crouched, about five feet two inches tall. He was thin and white-faced, resembling Mr Bizarre slightly. His deep but almost stupid eyes stared hard into the water as if in a trance, and his finger pointed directly where his eyes looked. His long robe was almost identical to the one Trouser was wearing, but it was a startling shade of green. It appeared to be luminous, and stood out like a beacon even in the surrounding greenery.

Trouser spoke almost in a whisper. 'Mm, yes, that's him. That's him. Now, be subtle here, don't want to alarm him. He's not altogether gregarious with strangers, but he'll come round in time, let me do the talking and memory mimicry. I should pull it off.'

Kurly Krishna the Kellogg Kid did not move a muscle as the party approached. They all sat or stood still in anticipation, even the jungle seemed tense and silent. The rubber boat floated just where Kurly Krishna's finger pointed, and the party saw that his head was bald and on it was printed a wonderful pattern, brilliantly coloured and intricate. His eyes were of a Hindu appearance, and his skin very pale and delicate. He could have been either ancient or very young. Trouser opened his arms in a friendly gesture and spoke: 'Kurly Krishna, baby! Nice to meet you again, hope we're here first. Are you

HEY LOOK! IT'S HIM!
SHHH!

HE'S IN A DEEP TRANCE WE MUST BE AS SUBTLE AS POSSIBLE...

THERE MUST BE A PSYCHIC TRICK SOMEWHERE
BLOOP!

PUFF!
PUFF!

WHEEZE

OORI
SH!

COR BLIMEY!
TURNED OUT NICE AGAIN 'AINT IT?!

coming out of your own accord or am I going to have to extract you, eh?'

The man did not move a muscle but remained like some huge heron waiting for its prey.

'Oh mate, 'ee looks dead to me,' said Dolse in Dil's ear.

'Shh. Quiet,' said Trouser with a finger to his mouth. 'He's in a deep, deep foliage trance, we shouldn't really disturb him but he could be here for weeks. Last time I saw him like this two stretcher bearers had to carry the bugger about for three days. It's not that he's anti-social or anything, he just likes to space out. And why not? It's easier than walking home.'

Tee Gee Trouser was silent and sucked his finger, still ignoring the robot quarter-snake wriggling on his wrist every time he moved. He scratched his golden hair which had grown curly again in the heat, and opened his dirty old raincoat. Sweat trickled behind his ears and streamed down his plump red face. He appeared to be thinking or pretending to.

Twiggott expressed the feeling of impatience among the others by polishing his boot with a big orangey-green leaf he'd picked up somewhere.

When Trouser spoke, it was more to himself than anything. 'Now let me see, aha . . . aha . . . there must be a psychic switch here somewhere, in fact,' he said with his vague blue eyes opening wide and staring forward, 'there must be a joke here somewhere.' He glanced quickly around the boat and then concentrated on the prostrate Kurly Krishna.

He took hold of Kurly Krishna's finger, and putting it in his mouth, began blowing hard, as if blowing up a balloon.

Indeed, to some of the crowd it seemed as if the strange man was growing in stature, or was it the life coming back to him? Yes, Kirly Krishna definitely was swelling up as Trouser blew up his finger. Suddenly the genius buffoon stopped blowing and shouted in his ear.

'Oouri Mata Burroosh! Oouri Mata Burroosh! Get the toadfish out of here!'

That did it. The statuesque figure blinked a while before stretching up straight and smiling wildly into Trouser's face. He stood for a moment and surveyed the people on the dinghy. Dil and Dolse almost holding hands and dressed in silver Biro suits. The cow snoring in her open box. Twiggott in his map of the world jump suit, and the Large Squad in purple banana suits with their numbers on the back and black pork pie hats perched on their heads. Rodney Shook looking startled as usual. Mr Straightly standing nervously with red knees covered in gnat bites, and Duffy Wigman, pissed out of his head, but looking quite sober and traditional. And Mr Bizarre, who the bald-headed Kurly Krishna looked on for some time approvingly. It was true, there was a remarkable resemblance between these two characters. Bruce had not returned.

'Blimey,' said Kurly Krishna, and they hadn't expected him to be a Cockney, 'watcha think yer doin' then? Wakin' me from me bleedin' evacuation stance, eh?' The voice was friendly and genial, but at the same time they all got the impression that they should have waited before awaking him.

Trouser's face looked a parody of apology.

'Tch, Gor lummy, what a shower you lot are, ent ya? You reckon this lots gonna hold their brain togever in outta space? Well, you're the kiddy, Trouser, you should know mate.' He looked up at the blue sky and flashes of sunshine filtering through the trees and vines.

'Turned out nice again, ain't it, turned out nice again.'

Chapter 15
The Turting Championships

Through the thick undergrowth on an almost invisible path they followed Kurly Krishna, the Kellogg Kid, cursing fake spider monkeys and beating off robot reptiles of bizarre description. The cow was not an easy travelling companion and Mr Straightly's corns were playing up. Scraping a sticky vine out of his face, he asked T.G. Trouser, who was directly ahead of him, about the canal.

'The canal? What Canal?' Trouser continued concentrating on following close behind Kirly Krishna who was unflurried by the joke animals screeching around them. (They had collected a large flock of plastic parrots by now, hopping from branch to branch.)

Mr Straightly frowned deeply and stumbled on behind him. He realized that the very idea of a canal, a green canal, starting nowhere and leading nowhere was absurd anyway, and he found himself agreeing with Trouser's obvious decision to forget the whole episode. He could not forget Bruce though, nor the beautiful Boloovial fish.

Quite suddenly, there was an old hoary brick wall to their left covered with very old English-looking ivy. The path grew wider and was now clearly visible as a deep red sand, and the jungle thinned out. They passed a huge tree which Mr Straightly immediately recognized as an oak from pictures he had seen back in England. Next there was a horse chestnut – a conker fell on Duffy Wigman's red head. Then there were some rhododendron bushes blooming in pink and white, and standing in the middle of one grew a palm tree, complete with coconuts.

'What the hell's happening here,' cursed Duffy Wigman grumpily. 'This wee Krishna chappie's a tree queer, ah dinna believe it if ah had nae seen it with ma oon eyes.'

And then, hardly perceptible at first but becoming increasingly enveloping, they heard the shrill whine of flutes and sitars, obviously played expertly and with great feeling. And there they stood, in a large sandy square on the perimeter of a town with yellow flat-roofed houses and date trees growing side by side with oak, ash, pine or sycamore, here and there between the buildings. There were people of all descriptions, either carrying food and children and looking busy, or sitting and watching the musicians, or playing themselves.

There was a fountain in the square spouting the green canal water and many people lazed around nearby, smoking much Pen-o-bip and laughing happily. To the right of the square, as you left the jungle wall, was a slight hill of lush green grass, stretching back a few hundred yards before it grew, quite sharply, into thick jungle again.

'Welcome to Javaal, me ole muckers,' said Kurly Krishna, turning and facing them. 'It's a bit on the old cosmopolitan side now, y'know. A few of yer wogs, a few froggies, a few Arabs an' stuff like. We original Javaalettes are a friendly bunch, know what I mean? People sorta wander in now an' again, just like yerself, Mr Trouser but unlike you, mate, they don't wander out again. But you always was a special case, weren't ya?'

Trouser gleamed and became animated. 'Now c'mon there Kurly, lay the sandwich on me, baby. What is it that keeps them here? Is it the below the belt activities, eh? Or the Pen-o-bip? I had trouble tearing my goodself away as I'm sure ya'll remember. I'm on the big one though, right? Got to follow destiny. Must reach my shining star; meet the crew.

The babbling Trouser introduced each one in turn to Kurly Krishna, especially Mr Bizarre. 'Staunch Trouserite and arch timber fancier,' said Trouser. 'I'm sure you two will get on like a glass camel.'

They were indeed naturally attracted to each other. It was a powerful meeting of minds. Bizer pulled out his infinity box and shot out coloured clouds which drifted around for a while in the hazy air, releasing raindrops of pretty water before they gradually dissipated. Kurly Krishna was duly impressed.

'Well blow me down!' said Kurly Krishna. 'Yer welcome 'ere mate, as long as yer like,' and then he led them through the square and into a luxurious temple where they got bipped and ate all manner of delicacies, fed to them by lovely dancers of dubious sex and nationality.

They slept (not entirely alone) in a luxury holiday chalet imported, plank by plank, from Bognor Regis and sandwiched between the temple and the Javaal unnatural history museum.

In the morning, Kurly Krishna, their guide and host, showed them around some of the sights and delights of Javaal. The Great Trouser surprised them all by turning out in full astronaut gear complete with helmet; the suit was a little tight around the stomach though.

'By Jesus, Trouser,' said Duffy Wigman, 'Ye must be sweating like a pig under that lot.'

Duffy himself wore a breezy transparent kilt and a sweat-stained Marks & Spencer's vest; he planned on relaxing whilst he was here.

'Oh just feeling it out, Duffy old son, getting the atmosphere of the situation,' replied Trouser with muffled words under the goldfish-bowl-shaped helmet.

They were all pleasantly overwhelmed on the remarkable Pen-o-bip substance which affected the human brain in ways no one had yet been able to analyse or even describe. Its strangest attribute though was its perfume. Under the influence of Pen-o-bip, which could be taken in a variety of ways, the human body would be flooded with a strange perfume that changed continually and could never quite be pinned down. The active constituent of the drug came from a strange plant that only grew in Javaal, it was called the Sturt Nebob, a ridiculous cross between the tea plant, hemp, venus fly trap and the spruce.

It was carefully cultivated by a team of Javaalette anti-scientists led by one Sturt Nebob Smith. A positive bark fancier and drug fiend. It was not all he was to develop either, and Javaal abounded with many strange life enhancers, some that made even Pen-o-bip look like Andy Pandy.

'Good old Sturt Nebob,' said Trouser holding his helmet under his arms as the group followed the smiling Kurly Krishna through a maze of carpet weavers and pretend basket makers. Trouser produced some rings of pineapple he'd saved from last night and offered a piece to their host.

He declined. 'No thanks, I'm anti-fruit.'

'Of course,' said Trouser, as if remembering.

Mr Straightly, always eager for new knowledge on the ways of the world, frowned in curiosity and made his way up to Kurly Krishna's side.

'By golly, Mr Kurly, sir, what's this anti-fruit business, if you don't mind me asking?'

'Anti-fruit?' he replied, leading the Trouser party around a bunch of eye dancers who were blocking a small alleyway. 'Not easy to explain at all, Mr Straightly, know what I mean? Well, y'know, like I got bitten by a trick strawberry once. I reckon that was the beginnin'. Bloody 'eavy scene the ole hostile fruit, I can't 'andle it these days, know what I mean?'

Mr Straightly smiled and scratched his shredded moustache. 'Mm, think I know the score. Bally terrifying the things that happen these days. Sometimes wish I was back in the Punjab, like my father, old war horse you know. Mind you, there are good things about these days. This Pen-o-bip stuff, a topping blitz, Bally good one, feel like a dream.'

Kurly gave Mr Straightly a piercing look at this last comment. 'I can see I'll have to watch you, mate, very carefully.'

Mr Straightly's face dropped for a split second as a cold tremble shot through his soul. He experienced something quite powerful and universal; a feeling of total paranoia. Kurly Krishna had hit him with it because he thought he needed it, just a flash. Then they both began laughing like drains. It started off slowly at first, just a trickle of smirking, and then built up until everyone was on the floor in hysterics. The place was a shambles of convulsions, there were belly laughs, mouth laughs, throat laughs, hoarse laughs, and girly giggles from the Biro Sisters. An alley full of people splitting their sides, grovelling in the red sand and more and more joining them all the time until there were hundreds. The alley was packed tight with people almost on top of each other trying to get in on the action, it was the sort of thing that happened all the time in Javaal. They had to be careful at times in case the whole country joined in at once; that could be a little dangerous.

'Gohh, ha! Jeezus, my compliments to the chef,' said Trouser, laughing loudly, hand over mouth. 'Remember the last time that happened, Kurly? When I was here I mean. I was trying to find a code phrase to get out of it.' He slapped Mr Straightly on the shoulder as the baffled man wiped his eyes with a nearby woman's robe.

'It's the non-fruit, Mr Straightly,' said Trouser in a loud voice. 'the anti-fruit laugh-out. Sponking great, isn't it? Real corkscrew tactics. Wow, where can I find a nutron pill?' Trouser smiled and sniffed as the crowd, still gurgling a little, slipped away.

'Yes, it's about time we noshed, I reckon, and time also for the Turting Championships. That should 'ave yer on yer backs. C'mon, this way,' said their guide.

They stumbled out of the alley following Kurly Krishna eagerly and had dinner in the Javaal Palace, where there seemed to be a tense air of excitement. Everyone in Javaal was getting keyed up for a major event. The Turting Championships.

It was hot afternoon when the Trouser party found themselves immersed in huge crowds of blitzed, colourful people heading for the massive Javaal arena. Pen-o-bip flowed freely, mostly in the form of smoking sticks. Twiggott and the Large Squad decided to travel on Javaal Moonheads: the strongest known hallucinogen on earth and only found in Javaal, where it was synthesised and made in pill form. Little transparent tablets that propelled the user not only into the already well-explored multiverse, but also through it, and into unknown indescribable realms, deep into the quintessence of super sub-sub atomic experience. It could not be unleashed upon the world at large. People just couldn't take it. Even Kurly Krishna had no answer to the phenomenon of a Moonhead 'Clown-out', as he called it. Only that it was a one-off journey into something that should only be spoken of in whispers. One thing he was certain of, a Clown-out was a decidedly alien feeling. Twiggott's startled eyes spun like big saucers; himself and the Large Squad had to be led through the crowds carefully and into the vast, but strangely intimate, arena.

As everyone took their seats, Kurly Krishna left the Trouser party on the front row and serenely walked to the centre pedestal. He flowed along like some graceful peacock in a 'Javaalette Dimension Robe' which appeared to have great depth and colour and changed shape continuously. He took the pedestal and immediately the people were silent. The atmosphere was almost eerie.

'Ladies and Gentlemen and inbetweens,' he said, beaming through his glazy eyes. 'There ain't much to say about turting that ain't been said already, know what I mean?' There was a flutter of applause. 'But we do 'ave some very distinguished guests in the audience today, all the way from England. And they probably wouldn't know a Turt from a glass centipede.'

More applause trickled through the hot hazy air.

'For those 'oo don't know, a Turt is a sound made with the ears. Like farting, but far more sophisticated and skilful. Why, we have people here in Javaal who devote their whole lives to it! And blimey, why not, eh?'

'Hurrah!' The crowd cheered massively.

'To Turt, one has to study inner space sound in great detail. Follow the vibrations right out to the extremities and channel them into the eardrums, thus controlling the cosmic rhythms with great finesse and patience. And, of course, for such an advanced practice, one has to be a positive anti-fruit. Well, back to me guests.' He looked towards the Trouser group. 'They are about to take on a dubious mission related to the strange occurrence that 'appened in Javaal just recently. They're gonna knock evolution on the 'ead for a bit and take the old corny plunge into outer space.'

A large 'Oooo' rippled through the crowd.

'Yeah, know what I mean, like? Personally speaking, I like where I'm at now and wouldn't join 'em for anything. But these brave people are spiritually and emotionally advanced enough to do the trip without any of the old competitiveness and argy bargy we used to 'ave in the old days before the big Blotto and the workers' uprising in 1984. On that premise, I wish 'em luck.'

This time the cheering really boomed and many people got to their feet, dancing wildly. They fell silent again suddenly when Kurly Krishna the Kellogg Kid coughed.

'But wait. That's not all, my people. I would like the leader of this mission to do a little announcin' for us this afternoon. Namely the names of the false competitors in this year's Turting Championships. I'd like the man 'imself to take the stand, being as he is a great performer and ruse creator of the first degree. Could we 'ave a monster hand please for – and BRACE YOURSELVES – the one and only, the abominable, the overweight, the bloody amazing, the electric Jesus himself, Mr T.G. TROUSER!!!'

The response was stunning. Poor Mr Bizarre had to block his ears at the deafening applause. Trouser, recognizing the near hysteria he had caused, dropped his space helmet, and made a dash for the pedestal, causing riots of laughter as his tubby body bounded for the centre.

He stood in the awed silence looking a little nervous. For a few minutes he spoke in Spanish, just for the hell of it. His silver space suit glinted like a new pin. He put on a pair of outsize purple sunglasses and took off the top of his suit. Underneath was a startling Hawaiian shirt with palm trees on it. He lit a green cigar and blew perfect smoke rings.

'It's hard to explain the feeling of numbness I have, stuck here, like a mutant bee breeder in a cyclone,' he said at last. 'I know nothing of Turting, but I do know a little about the solar possibilities within the human frame, after all, I am the pioneer of Music Therapy.'

That nearly brought the house down. They all knew how much the world owed to T.G. Trouser, the archbishop of inner space. He grinned madly in approval and tapped the cigar ash over the side of the plastic pedestal.

'We trudged wearily to this sacred secret country. Blocked on speed, sustained on nutron pills. Through quagmires and marshes, over mountains and summits, down glaciers and under water.' He was already well into an exaggeration pose; always good for a laugh – the crowd responded heartily.

'Through valleys of rotting pork! Between the vast gaping jaws of pre-pubescent timber monsters, up tall trees armed with man-gripper branches. Sometimes running, sometimes jumping, sometimes walking backwards; through hordes of opposition, but never . . . not never, doubting.' He slammed his hand on the top of the pedestal, his golden ring flashing brilliantly as the crowd stamped and cheered. So involved was Trouser that he mistook the crowd's cheers for jeers. He put his hands up in front of his face as if fending off pieces of rotten tomato.

'Without further ado, amigos, I shall lay the names of the false competitors on your considerable eardrums. Now dig this! First on the menu,' he screeched in a high pitched voice. 'A stereotyped buttress breeder of the first order, Mr Tout Legumes, take a bow, baby! And next, famous Javaalette eye dancer extraordinaire, Miss Hit! Shake them corneas, honeyrose.'

The applause for each contestant was long and passionate as they each stood up and revolved in costumes of great originality and splendour.

'The hot tip for the Turting title,' continued Trouser, 'is a young whippersnapper whose only credentials are the size of his parts, but he could be the one to walk out with the pseudo cup. Put them together please for Mr Machined Teeth! Thank you, thank you, friends. You may be wondering who the fellow in the outsized rubber bathing cap is, am I right?'

There was a large 'Noooo' from the crowd.

'Oh,' said Trouser, his face dropping. 'Suit yourselves. He is, of course, last year's champion Turter, a man of few words but a lot of laughs when the drink runs out. Mr and Mrs Smallpieces of Languid Tuber! Let 'im have it, please!!'

Rapturous applause and clouds of thick blue smoke lifted into the air. The sky was blue, the sun shone, and the excitement was scintillating.

If he was going out into space, Mr Straightly decided he would take a good suntan with him. So off came his shirt, shoes and socks, and on went his panama hat. Soon he was turning red and cripsy but, being too carried away by the proceedings, he didn't notice. He was, however, disturbed about the idea of a championship. It didn't seem at all civilized in an otherwise wonderful country like Javaal. He decided to ask Mr Bizarre for an explanation.

'I say, Mr Bizarre, old chappie,' said Mr Straightly, leaning across Duffy Wigman who had crashed out long ago. 'This damn Turting business. Is it really a bally competition? I mean does anyone win? It's all a bit barbaric. By thunder, I thought we'd had the last of that when Manchester United took to ballet dancing.'

Mr Bizarre stretched his gaunt neck outwards and started making croaking noises, somewhere between a bullfrog and a crane. He was wearing a PVC skull cap with a little English flag sticking out of the top of it. That was all Mr Straightly would get out of the top of it. That was all Mr Straightly would get out of him today, a series of croaks and plant imitations.

Meanwhile, Trouser was getting hot and sweaty and just about ready to stand down and enjoy the Turting. He made the final announcement 'Last but not least ladies and gentlemen, a pert character who hails from the north of Javaal where they call him 'the singing ear'. Let's have a big welcome please for Marty Stork an Organic Cork!!!'

Marty Stork an Organic Cork lifted his arms up high and wiggled his hips. He was a part-time Elvis Presley impersonator and was easily recognized by his ankle length watchstrap and two foot quiff.

The Turting had begun. There was hushed silence as the Turters, in order of announcement, did their stuff. There were many strange unearthly sounds echoing around the arena that day, all created through the highly sensitive eardrums of the competitors. Perhaps the most startling sounds were made by Marty Stork an Organic Cork who, by flexing his neck muscles, produced a noise like a flock of pink flamingoes taking to the air. The idea was to create perfect images in the minds of the spectators. The flamingoes were a novelty, seeing as they were now extinct, and 'the singing ear' nearly walked away with it.

LET THE TURTING CHAMPIONSHIPS BEGIN!
SURELY NOT A COMPETITION IN PEACEFUL JAVAAL!

I SAY MR. BIZARRE OLD CHAPPIE, IS IT **REALLY** A COMPETITION?!
CROAK?

..AND NOW.....**MARTY STORK!!**

COPYRIGHT © WILLY SMAX 1979

THIS YEAR THE CUP GOES TO.....
9 9 7 8 8 7 7
GRAND
TURTING
THEY'RE AWARDING A **CUP**,....HOW **BARBARIC!**

...**MISS HIT!**

But it was the beautiful Miss Hit who was finally awarded the pseudo cup by the panel of expert judges. She made a sound like a vast ocean, with rip tides and hurricanes and storm-tossed ships, finaly calming down to an ecstatic sunrise on the Caribbean, and fish and chips on Brighton pier. It was a breathtaking phenomenon, and even Mr Straightly was relieved to see that the prize was only a cracked antique paper cup. Miss Hit crushed it with her hand, proudly enforcing the new non-religion, Spannerism, which made a mockery of prize-giving and all the other rituals that go with it.

Spannerism's maxim was, 'all things are tools'. Even the greasy alcholic Scotsman, Duffy Wigman, thought he was in paradise during their stay in Javaal. But it was soon to be terminated; Trouser's destiny was propelling them forward into areas of tentacle importance.

The day burned away in merrymaking and entertainment. Rodney Shook and the Biro Sisters jammed with the local rock 'n' rollers, Rodney making a lovely improvisation especially for the event called, 'I'm gonna Turt ma head off honey.' It was a smash. Still barely returning from their Moonhead excursion, Twiggott and the Large Squad took the stage as the mirage light show replaced the sinking red sun. The Large Squad wore canary yellow banana suits and had their hair jet black and spiky. They stood around a microphone in black mock astros and crooned a harmony back-up while Twiggott sang a beautiful heartfelt version of 'Danny Boy'.

Dressed in a white satin suit and massive orange mock astros, Twiggott resolved never to kick another man, unless of course it was absolutely necessary. All the seats had been cleared away now. The evening was in full swing and the dim arena was a mass of writhing bodies, drinking, inhaling, and dancing around the see-through stage with its rose red background and huge prints of the exact design that adorned Kurly Krishna's bald head.

One of the highlights of the evening was when Mr Bizarre took the stage, dressed in pink carpet slippers, and candy striped pyjamas. The flag sticking out of his skull cap revolved as he recited a poem.

'Ahem,' he cleared his throat, and got stunning silence.

'A Peom.

And when I'm feeling real stripy, y'know? Zebra Vision.
Burned reptiles don't mean a thing
Cell fences frail in the wind
Deep pictures twist and bend
Happy couples eat each other under the laughing moon.

And what's all this peacock reaching?
Anybody like to buy a glass net?
Starched dummy's bobbing under foot
Crisp machines chewing nutty bolts
Mother turns into a clown
And blocks out everything that grins.

And when I flake crustily, y'know? Tinny strawberries.
Vast Gypsy's don't mean a thing
Bandaged streets need squeezing through
Past one dimensionals tasting blue
Before the mornings first saucy bottle.

And how about all this pillow sucking going on?
Seems stupid under a white eye
Blurting mouths threatening forever
Drop chocolate capsules endlessly.
Who left the tree in my eye?
Well, it was time I took my leaf (leave).'

It went down a storm. Even Kurly Krishna the Kellogg Kid snapped out of his spanner trance to catch the end of it and dragged Bizer back for an encore. At about 2 am Duffy Wigman lifted his head from heavy sleep to catch a glimpse of Mr Straightly on the stage swathed in orange light doing a knee dance. He dropped off again quickly with the silent thought that soon they would all be in orbit. He realized he had bitten off more than he could chew this time. He should have stayed with the 4th Dragoon Bagpipe Assembly. He knew that now, surrounded by exotic eye dancers who soaked in the ripples of the moon.

Chapter 16
A Wet Return

'We'd betta take some supplies, mate, it's a long way out of town. Sure ya won't stay a bit longer . . . just ta catch a few more anti-fruit laugh-outs?' Kurly Krishna was sitting on the stone edge of the fountain by the secret entrance to Javaal where the Trouser party had entered. In his right hand was a bowl of bark and soya soup which he spooned delicately into his mouth. He was wearing a cheap Japanese kimono. Trouser, sitting in a red and green deckchair wearing blue shiny shorts, a Javaalette anti-fruit T-shirt and a golfer's cap, stirred from a mild doze behind square white sunglasses. 'Umm . . . what?'

Kurly Krishna did not repeat the question but looked down on Trouser and his party, who were also lolling in deckchairs admiring the weather and the green water fountain.

Two black children played catch with a square ball and the slow bustle of the town sailed dreamily into their ears.

T.G. Trouser blinked as he took off the sunglasses and polished them on his naked dumpy red legs. His face was shiny and content and he pursed his round lips before he spoke. 'Ooooo, I don't think we can delay now, Kurly. The longer you stay, the stickier it gets. I think.'

There was a pause as he watched the children disappearing into the jungle to find their ball. 'Mayhap we'll be back, mayhap. Why . . . I might be back in the old Music Therapy business within months. There's still a need for it, you know.'

'I think you may be pushin' yer old luck, Trouser. They don't even know if it's gonna work, know what I mean?' Kurly Krishna put his bowl down onto the sand as he spoke.

Trouser continued: 'Well we'd best get up there and take a good eyeful. A few days milling around, some expensive idyllic artificial mountain air, a few old Brownie sing songs round a campfire and then . . .'

'And then what?' said Kurly a little cynically. 'Anyway,' he sighed. 'I'll go off and slip into somethin' a little more exquisite, like, and meanwhile you can get yerselves ready. I got a fleet of imitation Model T Fords all ready, we'll make it by late afternoon, awright?'

'Roger and out Major,' said Trouser, in an American accent.

Kurly Krishna stepped sprightly away into the town whistling 'Urban Spaceman' through his teeth.

Trouser was about to get up when Mr Straightly let loose a piercing yelp, sounding like a cross between a wild cat and a false parrot. He was standing leaning over the fountain in his brown plimsolls and khaki shorts, his thin legs shuddering. 'By thunder!' he yelled excitedly, beckoning Trouser. 'Mr Trouser, sir, he's back!'

Trouser jumped to his feet, dropped the white sunglasses onto the sand, and leaped towards the fountain looking shocked. He expected the worst, but was pleasantly surprised to see their old friend and travelling companion, his black shiny head sticking out of the water, grinning madly. His long whiskers dripped and his eyes were open wide and staring.

'Ee by 'eckers, this bloody water's starting to get uncomfortable. It's no good, I'll 'aff to get out.' Bruce, the seal-being, raised his black arm for a lift-out from Mr Straightly who obliged eagerly.

'Bally Bruce, old fish! Knew you wouldn't let the old school down, I'll fetch a towel.' He bounced away, grinning.

Bruce shook himself like a dog and spat and spluttered into the sand, looking down at himself as if disgusted at the soaking state he was in. The tuxedo he was wearing was sad and drooping and clung to him like wet black paper. 'Yeurk . . . look at that will yer, I've ruined me bloody trousers. I'll never get a crease like that in them again. Last time I go chasing women. Last bloody time. Where's me towel?'

Trouser looked throughtfully upon Bruce and rubbed his chin, nodding his head as if agreeing with a realization. He thought the creature looked more like a man than ever. His shape had changed in a subtle way and his pose was more two-legged. 'Well . . . well, well,' he said slowly, picking over the word.

'A' you stuck or somethin' mate?' said Bruce.

'Bruce,' said Trouser dramatically. 'You're welcome back to the fold. Any thought on space flight?'

'Eeee, I don't give three sponks mate. I just can't 'old me breath like I used to in the old days. Twenty minutes an' I'm choking like a bloody puffer-fish. I'm better out, I can see that.'

Twiggott and the Large Squad had left their deckchairs and were cheering Bruce and clapping around him. He felt good when he saw how happy they were to see him.

'Yoo old wombie yoo!' yelled Twiggott. 'Where's yer piece of salt den, eh? Whatcho bin up to, Brucey? Back fer good is yer?' He put a brotherly arm around Bruce and shook him, plonking a special anti-fruit skull cap, given to him by Kurly Krishna, on to the sealman's head. The cap came down over his eyes and pushed his ears outwards. Bruce started giggling happily. 'Yer a bloody berk and an 'e', Twiggott, a bloody berk. But yer alright mate, yer alright! Can I get a pint 'ere, eh?' He looked over at the flat-roofed houses of Javaal. 'Eee bloody 'ell, looks a right mousetrap does this place, when are we leavin'?'

'Any minute now, Bruce,' said Trouser. 'Just follow my arse.'

Mr Straightly returned with a white towel with the words 'The Dorchester' printed on it in black letters on one of the corners. Bruce rubbed himself down as they walked slowly across the square.

Trouser led the way to the Javaal Palace for a last meal before they took to the hills.

Chapter 17
Chutney, Collins and Milton

There was joviality and laughter in the luxurious Javaal Palace that morning as they drank bee wine from mock coconut shells with the famed Kurly Krishna design printed on them. Over a smoke of Pen-o-bip, Bruce told the tale of his affair with the Boloovial fish.

'Aye, she was a right one alright. Not a bad piece of scale in her own way, like. Bloody pretty eyes, I'd of married her too if it wasn't fer the obvious.'

'What do you mean Bruce old chap, what happened?' asked Mr Straightly.

'It's a short story really, Mr Straightly, but I'll try an' exaggerate, just fer entertainment's sake and 'cos I'm bipped out of me mind. It 'appened like this. We were 'angin' the cats out to dry one night – she kept a couple of underwater robot moggies, fer company like – when she started comin' over all queer. All introvert sort of. Wouldn't answer when I asked if she wanted anything for tea. She just turned away from me, and she kept on looking down at 'er tail. I said, "what's up love? What's bugging' yer like, yer look a bit pale." '

'Ah . . . excuse me Brucey, ah hope yoo dinna mind me buttin' in like this,' said Duffy Wigman, leaning across the table with a cup of bee wine in his hand and a few nutron pills crackling between his yellow teeth. 'But, ah, where did ye live? Not in that wee stinking green cesspool, ah canny believe it. Why . . . the banks o' the place was as smooth as my arse cheeks, you couldnay git a homely atmosphere in a place like that, could ye now?' Duffy had a way with words.

Bruce creased his lips realizing Duffy Wigman just could not understand true love. 'Yer bloody daft Duffy, daft as yer sporran. We, if you really want to know, we lived in an old cockpit of a bloody great jumbo jet that 'ad somehow found its way into the canal. It was quite cosy, just me an' 'er. Sittin' back, twiddlin' with the controls. Eee by 'eck, I would have loved to hijack that big plane when she was doing a regular schedule.'

'Bruce!' said Trouser. 'How did you know about Jumbo jets? You weren't around when they were the mode of travel. C'mon, lay the sandwich on me.' Trouser was wearing a black eye patch as he spoke.

'I've read the brochures, Mr Trouser. Oh yes, I've read the lot. Apart from that, there was all kinds of old bits of aeroplanes lying around in the sea when I was a lad, if you understand me like. Anyway . . . where was I? Oh aye. This one day she was all sort of remote and sad, the Boloovial fish, I mean. I just couldn't get more than a few squeaks out of her and then it 'appened.'

They all stared at Bruce expectantly.

He chewed some vegipills and swilled them down with bee wine. 'She ate 'erself,' he said soberly.

'She ate herself?' repeated the others.

'I mean she ate 'erself. Simple as that. I told you Boloovial fish eat themselves, and that's what she did. She just curled over suddenly, like a hedgehog curling up, and she put 'er tail in 'er mouth and started chewing. Eee, bloody turned me up, it did. Soon as it was over I was straight up on t'bank and throwin' up like a good 'un, Christ.'

'But Bruce, I say, old stick . . . ah' it was Mr Straightly having one of his dithering attacks. The facial twitching had returned again, he was falling apart.

'D . . . didn't you try to . . . ah . . . stop her from eating herself? I mean, it's all well and good if a chap wants to take his own life. I can't stand anymore, end it all, bally ho and what have you, but eating yourself? I say . . . it's a bit strong isn't it?'

'Well, that's as may be, Mr Straightly, but that's what Boloovial fish do, an' I did try to stop 'er. But every time I made a grab to separate 'er mouth from 'er tail, she just spun like a bloody top. Couldn't get a grip on the little bugger anywhere.'

He paused, sighing, eyes downcast into the wine shell and whiskers drooping like weeds.

'So . . . before long she just . . . vanished like. Gone. No more, no more at all. Started from the tail and worked 'er way up. Pop!'

There was sudden laughter as Four'ser, of the Large Squad, fell backwards onto the floor like a tree, bellowing with laughter and holding his stomach.

'It's no bloody joke,' said Bruce indignantly, and then he chuckled a little. 'She didn't even put any salt on.'

Three'ser and Two'ser had by now dropped off their stools and were grovelling in fits of laughter on the thick red carpeted floor. And it wasn't long before the whole Trouser party were splitting their sides, including Bruce.

'It's no good crying over eaten Boloovial fish, is it?' he said.

They laughed long and wildly until Kurly Krishna appeared, pointing out that it was time to leave.

Their extra baggage had gone on ahead and the Trouser party stumbled out of the Javaal Palace, surrounded by well wishers, and into the fleet of Model T Fords, or at least reasonable facsimiles.

Only the cow was missing. That very morning she had been observed rushing headlong into the jungle after someone had inadvertently fed her a stick of Pen-o-bip. Trouser was at first deeply disturbed by this incident, but brightened up somewhat when he realized it was probably all for the best. 'Three Points to the Home Team' had been eating like a horse just lately – a bad habit for a cow to get into, Trouser reasoned.

It was a bumpy journey and all uphill but the scenery was pleasant. There were little hamlets and villages where they stopped for refreshment and entertainment. Someone would usually do a few brain tricks for their amusement and Rodney Shook always had some instrument for accompaniment. There were remarkable plant shows, and all kinds of tree appreciation took place. Kurly Krishna didn't like to see bored people so he gave each a 'Circuit Stamp' non-gun for shooting tin monkeys and all forms of false animals that they happened to come across. The special guns were aimed at the phony creatures and acted directly on their circuits, making them go dead for a few minutes. Then they would pop up again and carry on as normal. It was skilful and it passed the time.

Trouser was very quiet. He sat in the back of the leading Model T Ford with Duffy Wigman and made peculiar facial expressions, as if acting out some inner drama. Duffy Wigman had run out of alcohol and the Pen-o-bip was finally getting to him. His yellow eyes rolled and his teeth felt like splinters of wood in a desert. After a while on the road, he broke into some explicit pornographic songs, flipping his pubic sporran up in time to the beat. Rodney Shook refused outright to join in, stressing that he was a soul brother and an artistic idealist would not associate himself with such a bullshit man. Duffy retaliated by saying he looked like a broomstick in a bush. It didn't get a lot of laughs and soon the whole business was very twentieth century, but they quickly calmed down as the road got tougher.

It was very hot and there was nothing but broken rocks and sand on either side of them. The only break in the scenery for at least ten miles was the sudden appearance of vast pastures of the plant Sturt Nebob from which came the wonderful brain tool, Pen-o-bip. The fields formed narrow strips stretching away to the horizon on either side of the road. The plants were about five feet tall and many shades of green and they seemed to move of their own accord, rippling like corn in the wind, for as far as the eye could see.

As soon as the Pen-o-bip pastures had been left behind, the broken landscape continued for some miles until, quite suddenly, they found themselves surrounded by high stone walls, sheer faces of mountains with strange colourful mosses growing through cracks in thick clusters, casting long shadows in the afternoon heat. The Model T Fords picked their way carefully along the rather treacherous road like strange metal insects.

When the mountain range was left behind, the scenery took a definite turn for the better. The road opened out and pine trees grew tall and strong. There was a positive English feel about the place, and the startling appearance of a 1970 council house seemed by no means incongruous. It was a typical estate model with the usual box-like shape and white painted window frames with a sick blue door. It was number 11, Javaal extremity road. Quite a nice area.

They pulled up outside the door and Kurly Krishna knocked loudly. It was very quiet. Like a Sunday afternoon. Bruce scuffled his feet in the sand outside the house and peered in through the lace curtain windows, but he could see nothing.

There was no garden, just yellow sand.

Kurly Krishna knocked louder and eventually someone in the house moved and the door opened. Standing there was a tall man with short black hair and sharp, dark features. He smiled widely over big white cannonball teeth. He wore an off the peg Italian style blue suit with a white cotton shirt and a thin pale blue tie.

'Vecome! Velcome, Kurly Krishna! Come and have ze cup of Engleesh tea.' He looked at Trouser and the motley gang. 'Aha . . . and zis must be ze famed T.G. Trouser, no? I am deeply honoured to meet you, sir, please accept my humble hospitality. I am one of ze few remaining Russians on ze planet earth. I am Hatpin Degenovitch, space engineer and smooth metal object fetishist. Do come in, zis way, please.'

He beckoned them in and soon they were reclining in the canary yellow and gooseberry green sitting room, drinking tea.

Kurly Krishna asked Trouser to follow him into the kitchen where Hatpin Degenovitch was making a second pot. The gaunt Russian's blue tie matched the floor tiles. When he spoke, it sounded as if he had learned English from a long playing record, but it was passable.

'Mr Trouser,' he said, slickly tugging at his white shirt cuffs. 'You do not know how exciting zis is for me. Why it is my dream to haf a successful lift-off, something that has so far eluded me in my thirty or more years in space travel. Oh, I haf had plenty of satellites and missiles, you know? But zay are so boring, so dull and antiquated . . . a man could waste his life. More tea?'

'Mm, yes please, Mr Degenovitch, it's a cool brew you make here, must be the mountain air,' said Trouser.

'How many sugars?' said Degenovitch.

'Fifteen,' said Trouser.

'Fifteen, I see, oh ve must not be formal now, must we? Please call me Hatpin.'

'Very well,' said Trouser. 'Please call me Captain Zoom, Chip Throwupp, or Mr Swaddling keys to the boot.' He produced his circular comb. 'Or just Mr Trouser if you know what's good for you.' He smiled strangely as he flicked the comb over his golden locks.

'Of course,' said Hatpin Degenovitch, pouring hot water into a metal tea pot. 'I take it you haf seen ze ship ven you were here last? I was out of Javaal collecting a few important items, as I'm sure our good Kurly Krishna here has informed you.'

Kurly Krishna was picking around in the fridge.

'I am sure you vill be ze perfect astronaut, Mr Trouser, you are probably best equipped of all earthmen for this mission, but I am not so sure about your crew. Are zey all going with you?' He handed Trouser a green cup of tea.

'What the pank?' said Trouser, shocked, as he looked into his tea cup. 'This tea's green. What's the meaning of this?'

'No no no,' said Degenovitch hastily. 'It is just the reflection of ze cup.'

'Whew,' said Trouser blinking and taking a sip of the steaming brew. 'Thought I was having a relapse for a minute there,' he said relieved.

'Ah . . . ze 1986 green vision, am I right?' said Degenovitch.

'Of course,' answered Trouser. 'Now, getting back to the crutch of the matter, Mr Degenovitch, getting back to the ultimate dirtbox of the situation, to the cork and grind as you boffins might say . . . I'd like to know if we're going to leave the ground, etc.'

'Vell, according to ze weather analysis and other scientific data which would probably go above your head, she, the ship, should at least leave our solar system, with, how you say? comparative ease.'

'Comparative to what?' asked Trouser snappily.

'Comparative to jumping,' said Degenovitch with a clean grin.

MORE TEA MR.TROUSER?
AH YES PLEASE MR. DEGENOVITCH

I'M SURE YOU WILL MAKE ZE **PERFECT** ASTRONAUT

THIS TEA IS GREEN!

NO! IT'S JUST ZE **REFLECTION** OF, OF ZE **CUP!!**
THANK GOODNESS! I THOUGHT I WAS HAVING A **RELAPSE!**

AH!... ZE GREEN VISION OF 1986?
OF COURSE
SLURP!

'Hm, yes, that seems both satisfactory and olfactory, mein scientific adviser. Good. Good. Let's not delay then. Show me the module controls and give me the fitness tests and whataveyou, and we'll be off by tomorrow tea-time.' Trouser cracked the cup down on the saucer and put it in the false china sink.

'Fitness tests?' said Degenovitch. 'Fitness tests. Mr Trouser?' There is no need for this sort of carry-on these days. The space ship has been modified beyond recognition. Let me assure you, you look plenty fit to me.' The Russian clasped his hands together in a satisfied manner.

'No fitness test? Tch . . . what a pity, what a great pity. I was hoping for a good work-out on the parallel bars and such like, get a bit of the old self-indulgent flab off. Just for the hell of it. What about brain tests? Familiarizing with states of non-gravity. Stress and strain on the spatial relationships and you name it. No?'

'No, sorry,' said Degenovitch sadly.

'Not even a little . . . ah, mind altering experience before we go; no?'

'No, sorry,' said Degenovitch. 'There's surely no need.'

'Not even an itsy bitsy portion of Moonhead to see if I can take the strain? No? Ah well, pity, pity. Thought I might get one in before lift-off. Still we'll take a good supply, in case we have to fool ourselves that we're not really up there if things do start going wrong. Okay, baby, let's press on, lead me to the next phase.' T.G. Trouser minced out of the kitchen. He was wearing a tight pair of beige shorts and the top half of a space suit.

About three-quarters of a mile behind the council house, in a valley black and scarred by its landing, stood the tall silver spaceship, Apollo XXIIII. It was surrounded by cool misty mountains and beyond the blackened area grew small shrubs and grass and scattered belts of pine trees. The ship stood on four arched legs that reached a quarter of its height and about half-way up was the American flag emblem. To its right (about half a mile away) tucked under the overhanging ridge of a mountain, was a long flat-roofed control building with a huge radar scanner by its side like a big fly's eye.

The party left the Model T Fords and stood on a grassy crest admiring the view. After a while Hatpin Degenovitch asked them to follow him on foot down over the grass and onto the blackened plain to the spaceship. The day was very hot but not uncomfortably so. They passed sticks of Pen-o-bip as they walked.

The fifteen people ambled between the legs of the spaceship and stared up at it in silence. It certainly looked capable of making a long flight through space and Trouser was satisfied with everything so far. He looked over at the control building and revolving radar scanner shimmering through the heat haze.

'Shall we check out the button pushers, Hatpin?' he said.

'Vel, ve can in a moment, but there is something else I'm sure you vill be interested in. Come zis way everybody, pleese.'

They followed the slick scientist Degenovitch across the charred earth to a nearby copse. It had a desolate feel to it, pine trees and mounds of sand with thin grass and small strange bushes grew as if defying the presence of the ruin the spaceship had caused on its landing.

The pine needles crackled as they walked through the copse and when they emerged on the other side, they were confronted by a most interesting spectacle. For sitting between two big pale boulders on yellow sand were three men, dressed in tattered silver spacesuits. Two of them were immersed in a game of cards, the other one ate what looked like hot baked beans which he spooned out of a space helmet. They all had fair hair croped short in crew cuts and stubble grew on their jaws.

They looked up in bemusement at the sudden appearance of this strange group of people. The one with the beans dropped his spoon in his helmet and stood up extending his hand. He spoke in a healthy American drawl.

'Well, I'll be doggone! Yihaa! If'n we ain't been found at last! Ma name's Chutney, Captain Chutney, and these here are ma comrades, Captain Collins, an' Flight Lieutenant Milton. An' we hereby claim this planet in the name of the United States of America.' He proudly pointed to an erected American flag and then standing to attention, saluted proudly. The others stood up and saluted likewise, then Degenovitch shook hands with all three men. He introduced himself and T.G. Trouser, and the Americans said, 'Nice to meet ya'll.'

'Hey' said the blue-eyed Captain Chutney. 'Ya'll folks look jus' like earthmen, it sure is a humdinger! Why if I didn't know any better I'd say that we was right down there back on ole planet earth again, yessiree. Yihaa!' He slapped his side wildly. The others nodded agreement. They were obviously totally mad.

'Ah, yes, vell . . .' said Degenovitch hesitantly. 'You see gentlemen . . . actually, you are back on earth. Quite near Tibet actually. Velcome to Javaal.'

Degenovitch put his hand up and said to the wide-eyed Trouser from the side of his mouth, 'says he, as if I haven't said it at least a dozen times before.' He looked back at the astronauts quickly and smiled toothily.

'Yes, yes, of course, gentlemen. There's no need to explain. You haf lost your vay due to faulty controls, the space ships of the 1980s were not too reliable, no?' It was obvious to the astute mind of Trouser that he was humouring them. But what was the ruse, he thought.

'If I may butt in,' said Trouser, as the Americans looked increasingly confused and scratched their cropped hair. 'Captain Chutney, Captain Collins, Flight Lieutenant Milton.' He addressed them each with a nod. 'What year was it when you blasted off?'

Collins scratched his jaw. 'Why . . . it was 1981 when we's first lifted from ole Houston, 1981.'

'Uhum . . .' said Trouser. 'And what, pray tell me, what year is it now?'

'Why it's, wait a minute, I'll just get ma lil' ol' chart.' Collins stepped behind one of the boulders and returned with a log book. Degenovitch smiled knowingly at Trouser.

'The year, in earth time, is . . . let me see now . . . yeah. It's 1983. That's it,' he said, looking at Trouser. '1983.' He placed the book down onto the sand.

'Hey, what is this anyways? If'n we's really back on earth, youse is the strangest lookin' recovery crew I ever clapped eyes on. What gives here, buster, huh, what gives?'

Degenovitch spoke. 'The year, gentlemen, is 2073. Please do not be

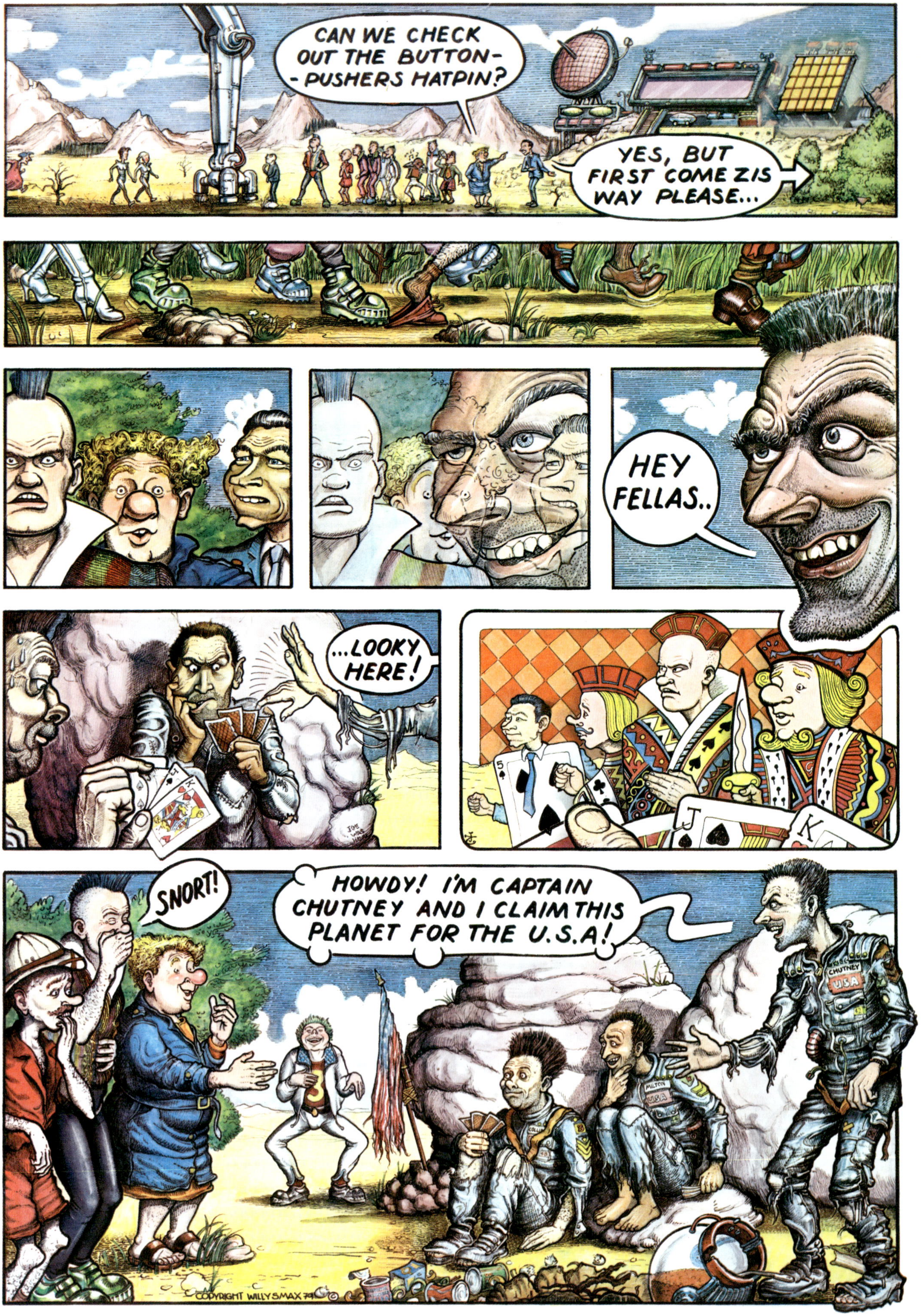

HEY FELLAS..

...LOOKY HERE!

alarmed, there has been a slight cosmic mishap. Nothing to worry yourselves about, please accept our humble hospitality. Velcome back.'

Chutney exchanged panicky glances with the other two crew members. 'Why that's just about the damned craziest thing ah ever heard in my entire thirty-one years! Look buddy. If'n that there's true . . . why . . . what about ma lil' wife an' kids down in Texas with our lil' ranch? An' what about the President of the Yoonited States, huh. Don't tell me they's all dead an' buried!'

'Vell, my good man. The President is most definitely dead and buried, but your vife . . . that may be another matter. People live much longer nowadays you know. Largely due to our friend Mr T.G. Trouser and his Music Therapy treatment. But I am afraid your little ranch down in Texas is most probably, how you Americans say? Vamooshed, no? America is mostly populated by dolphins now, they evolved some years ago, cute creatures dolphins, don't you think?'

The Americans couldn't stomach it. 'Dolphins?' they said.

'Music Therapy? Dolphins? T.G. Trouser? Nah . . . nah, look here. Ah don't know what your game is pal, but ah want a recovery crew out here pronto! Ya'll undersatnd? Pronto.' Chutney was exasperated. He stomped around looking at them. He stopped in front of Twiggott and looked him up and down. Twiggott wore black tights, emerald green mock astros, an orange T-shirt and a fluorescent multi-coloured jacket. His hair was blood red and stood up like a bush on fire. He eyed the astronaut coolly with a smirk on his full lips.

'Jesus Christ!' said the American.

'Almost,' said Twiggott, folding his arms. The Large Squad, all in yellow banana suits, stepped a little nearer.

'Ah, c'mon now. Ah know. Ahhh know, don't tell me . . . you're makin' a movie. Hot diggity! Youse making a movie, right?'

'Don't come da wombie wiv me, hotdog,' said Twiggott dryly.

'Wha's your name pal, huh?' said the mad astronaut.

'Twiggott,' said Twiggott.

'Twiggott?' said the Captain. He then looked over at Mr Bizarre who was smoking his special mixture, completely absorbed in the scene.

'Ah . . . an' you buddy, you with the robe. Wha's your name?'

'Mr Genital Disorders,' answered Mr Bizarre without moving.

'Twiggott! Trouser! Degenovitch! Mr . . . Genital Disorders?! Why, youse fuckers ain't even got proper names, goddamnit! Ah don't accept this at all. Ah don't accept it!' He went back to Hatpin Degenovitch and pointed a finger at him accusingly. 'Now you look here, Tiepin – or whatever you say your name is – you come back here with a United States recovery team, an' a camera crew, an' . . . an' a red carpet, an' you go . . . go now, an' get them here an' tell them that the 1981 solar probe mission has done come back! Ya'll understand?'

'Perfectly,' sighed Degenovitch. 'Long live America, they will be on their vay presently.'

'Okay pal, you better see to it,' said Chutney, returning to his baked beans.

The other two sat down with their backs to the rock and looked vaguely around them. Within seconds they were totally ignoring the Trouser party, who, at Hatpin's request, turned away and walked back through the thin pine trees.

Chapter 18
Forward With Both Feet

As they scuffled along in silence, Twiggott thought he heard a strange animal-like sound coming from a clump of bushes just on the other side of the pine trees. He veered off to investigate and just as he reached the shrubs, a small bird-like creature dashed off across the charred ground in the direction of the spaceship. The others watched as Twiggott, skull cap in hand, chased the strange brown bird which made a loud frightened clucking sound. Twiggott laughed in amusement and called out to Trouser, asking if he knew what it was. Trouser was a little uncertain but Degenovitch said it was a thing called a chicken. Something the astronauts had taken with them on their journey for scientific experiments to see how it would cope with space flight. It seemed as mad as the astronauts, fluttering around, sometimes rolling over and over in a ball in an effort to escape Twiggott.

'Hatpin,' said Trouser after some pause. They were nearing the control building and could already see signs of life behind its windows. 'Chutney, Collins and Milton: what do you, as a smooth metal object fetishist and near genius scientist, what do you make of it? Am I right in thinking they've been out there a long time?'

Degenovitch sighed and raised his hands for a moment, letting them drop again limply against his thighs. 'It is a great pity vot has happened to those three . . . I . . . I cannot fully explain it myself. But time and time again I have tried to get them to haf some help, understand? But vill they accept help? No . . . no they vill not. Every time I get the same old spiel from them. Bring a recovery team, they say. Demanding this, demanding that, ohh! It is no use. They will probably not even notice ven you take off in their ship.'

Degenovitch loosened his collar, panting a little in the heat. Two silver doors automatically opened as they reached the control building and they stepped inside.

'Whew,' said Degenovitch. 'It seems hotter than ever now and it vill soon be dusk. Vot is the right time, Mr Trouser, pleese, haf you got it on you?'

Trouser spoke quietly as if to himself. 'Yes, what is the time?'

In a large room full of control panels and computers, Degenovitch introduced Trouser to some of his staff. There was Mint Corpuscle, the thin bespectacled atomic fuel expert delirious. Spangle Slab, an ex-gorilla matchmaker now turned professional floor sweeper and important piece of scrap paper finder. He was a skinny youth whose legs seemed joined together from the knees up. There was Miss Definite Sexual Attraction, a lady who never said no for an answer. And also a hideous computer programmer who did Bette Davies impersonations in her spare time.

Trouser was pleased with the staff, he felt he was in capable hands. For most of that evening they all got zombied and discussed the mission. From the food to the fuel they talked long into the night, leaving no stone unturned and no detail undelved.

Lift-off was to be at about tea-time the next day, provided they all woke up in time. Just one thing was bothering Mr Straightly. How were they going to get into the ship? The hatch was a long way up. He posed the question to Hatpin Degenovitch who said, 'Ho, it is quite simple, we haf a ladder.'

Mr Straightly twitched nervously for a while and then fell into a deep sleep. They carried him off to bed and he awoke at mid-day, September the 23rd, 2073, to the sound of, 'Space ain't no place for de human race but who done make de rules anyway?' It was Rodney Shook with the Biro Sisters, wailing out his latest composition in the commune room. Mr Straightly jumped out of bed and joined in on tambourine and harmony vocals. He was becoming quite a little groover, but Trouser had his eye on him.

Outside, the space ship was being checked thoroughly and loaded with provisions and all manner of equipment, hopefully ensuring the Trouser expedition a reasonably comfortable journey through space. After the rock and roll session they boarded the ship with Hatpin Degenovitch for an inspection tour. Inside the massive machine they found much more than they had ever bargained for. Degenovitch had certainly done a good job.

There was a large relaxation room with pin tables, rat-splatters, slide projectors, and hundreds of films. A bar, a small imitation wood stage for Rodney Shook, robot tropical fish in a huge tank that took up the whole of one side of the room; and it was all fitted out with lush wall to wall purple carpeting and maroon chairs and settees. Every single room, compartment and corridor was graced by its own stereo tape equipment and the record library went right back to 'Be-bop-a-lula'. Every cabin was a different colour and was as luxurious as anything in the saucerette line. The store room was done in cool steel and had cabinets full of bottles and jars of pills, capsules and crystals of every known medicine and intoxicant under the sun. Ther were vast perspex containers holding millions of Music Therapy Vacopods and a separate storeroom for the Javaal Pen-o-bip.

It certainly was decked out in style and even the main control room at the head of the ship was relaxing with its natty botte green and tangerine finish.

They looned around becoming accustomed to the controls; Degenovitch was all grins and pride.

'Good good good,' bellowed Trouser, buffooning with the dials and switches. 'I certainly admire the damn fool who did this little lot out.' He looked up at the paintwork. 'Bastard must have thought we were going on a bloody picnic! Bloody good service I call it, Hatpin my lad, where's the pisser? I'm bursting.'

'So glad you are pleased, Mr Trouser. It is down to you now, it is down to you to take mankind outwards into new heights of idiocy. I do hope everything vill go according to . . . vell, according to vatever vill happen.' Degenovitch clasped his hands together well chuffed with himself.

'Hm, okay, Degenovitch, don't let it go to your head. Who the hell's paying you anyway? Get off and let me take this baby upwards, can you dig it?'

'Yehess . . . good Mr Trouser, I see you are in fighting form, no? I vill take my leave and vish you good luck. Ohh, and don't forget to keep in radio contact. Goodbye and good luck, all of you.' Degenovitch clicked his heels and left them in the control room.

'Well, it's a sad farewell from me, mate, best of luck ta ya, though. And that goes for everyone in Javaal. Take care.' It was Kurly Krishna, a concerned look on his thin white face as he shook hands with Trouser. Trouser was still watching the Russian as he disappeared through the door.

'Mm? Oh right. Thanks, Kurly honeyrose. Thanks for everything. Watch that Degenovitch man though, just for me, eh?' said Trouser confidentially. 'I think he's a bit too slick for his teeth, understand?'

He didn't, but nodded encouragingly.

Kurly Krishna the Kellogg Kid shook hands with everybody and bade them a fond farewell. Bruce tried to persuade him to come along for the trip but he wouldn't leave Javaal, it was too close to his brain, he said.

There was really no need, but T.G. Trouser insisted on them all wearing space suits for the take-off. He produced a miniature camera and took a few snapshots of them. Trouser took his helmet off to make radio contact with base: 'Trouser speaking, Trouser speaking. Now how do we get this tube off the ground, does anybody know?'

There was a slight crackle as Degenovitch answered. 'You vill find a red button on the control panel in front of you, Mr Trouser, it says "Start" quite clearly. Can you see it?'

Trouser looked at the dials and buttons in front of him until he found the big red button. He poised his bloblike finger over it.

'Yes, ground control, I've found it, it's right here. Now, do I press it or what?'

'First you must all strap yourselves in the chairs provided,' said Degenovitch. They all did what he said.

'A OK Hatpin, old sugar, A OK. Do we have lift off?' Trouser had been watching too many old movies.

'Just press the button, Mr Trouser, Bon Voyage,' said Hatpin.

'A OK. Adios, Roger Handout, Roger Handout.'

T.G. Trouser nervously pressed the red button on the silver control panel and they were away. There was a powerful vibration that seared through their minds and bodies for the first few seconds and a judder as if an earthquake had hit them. But all in all, it was a smooth lift off. Off came their space suits and on came the stereo. Twiggott selected the revised version of 'Flying Saucers Rock 'n' Roll' by the Crabshell Polishers; it seemed fitting. Dil and Dolse, however, at the thought of space travel, got all romantic and said they would much rather have 'Fly me to the Moon'.

'Don't be soppish,' said Twiggott. 'We ain't goin' to da bleedin' moon.'

It was what you'd expect from those two though, they were a remarkably smarmy pair. They both wore light green plasticy congress suits with matching mascara.

Duffy Wigman stood in front of the ten video screens and stared at the one that showed the earth. It was already visible and quite clearly they were gathering tremendous speed. His mind wandered back to his childhood in Almost Scotland; his father's little porridge shop on the corner, Molly McTavish, the first girl he ever de-pubed for his amazing sporran. And wonderful Loch Ness, where he used to go with a gang of friends every year skin-diving and dragging dummy monsters just under the surface to keep the tourists coming. He rubbed his bloodshot leathery face throughtfully as Planet Earth became smaller and smaller on the screen. Mr Straightly joined him, frowning, as if he too were deep in nostalgia.

'By George,' he said with emotion. 'It's going to take a damned lot of beating, old Planet Earth, it may have its bally problems, but it's home.'

'Aye,' said Duffy Wigman. 'Wee'll not see a better place than bonny Scotland when Hogmanay is upon us. We'd have te search the whole wee canny corners o' the universe to find a place like it. Och! How the heel did I get myself in this bloody mess?'

'Oh, come now, old chap, stiff upper and all that, stiff upper! Keep the old school walking, what! We'll show those Martians and whathaveyou how it's done, by thunder. We'll show them how the British carry on!'

Mr Straightly saluted the screen fiercely. Earth was a pretty marble in a blue ocean by now. He twirled his limp moustache and smiled proudly at the Scotsman who sneered back at him. 'You must be pankin creezy man, pankin' creezy,' and he turned and walked off to examine another control panel.

'I say . . .' said Mr Straightly.

There was nothing much for any of them to worry about as far as running the ship was concerned, it more or less ran itself. The course had to be set though, and Trouser had no idea as to which route they should take. He was continually changing his mind as they left the earth's atmosphere but decided it would be nice to take a peek at Venus.

Only one thing was bothering Trouser as he set the controls and put the ship on automatic pilot; Apollo XXIIII was a bit of a dour name considering the importance of the mission. He must give it some thought. He took the lift down to the relaxation room and had a quick pin table tournament with Bruce who was involved in the timeless struggle of evolution. Every time the seal-being looked into the giant robot tropical fish tank, he had a powerful urge to jump right in there and have a flounder about; but he was rigidly determined not to let this get the better of him, knowing full well it would be uncomfortable and probably retard the process of destiny.

Trouser stretched out on a deep maroon settee, smoking a fat orange cigar containing various substances. Bruce joined him.

'By gum, Trouser, they've done us proud with this tin can, eh. Eee, I'd hijack this piece of junk if I found it lying around, I can tell yer, bloody 'ell.' Bruce stuck the cigar up his nose and inhaled.

'Yes,' said Trouser, idly picking the settee. 'She's a mean experience alright. But what the sponk are we going to call her? That's my only complaint. Any thoughts on the matter, Bruce, eh? Any gems?'

The door slid open and Twiggott stepped in, followed by One'ser and Two'ser, Bruce gave the cigar to Two'ser who thanked him several times.

'Well, I don't know, I really don't,' said Bruce, smoke streaming out of his nose and through his whiskers. 'Why not call it . . . Trouser Houser? Or meybe, eh meybe, Trouser's last jump, eh?'

'No, it hasn't got that ring to it, it must have that ring.' Trouser blinked vaguely and started clacking his teeth together. He jumped to his feet with a start and, pointing his finger upwards, screamed, 'I've got it! It's come through.'

'What'as boss,? Whatcha gonna call it?' said Twiggott.

'Eee panking Christ!' said Bruce. 'You scared the bloody scales off me then mate . . . Christ.'

'I'll call it,' steamed Trouser, 'it shall be known as: Neat Vampires at Half Price (apply within).'

It had a ring to it, they all agreed on that; but whether or not it would bring them luck was another matter. In the blackness of space they had already been perilously close to colliding with several old earth satellites that had been spinning around for years. Mr Straightly spent hours watching the junk that earthmen had sent up flashing across the video screens. He ducked and closed his eyes many times when it looked like a collision. There seemed, however, something of a magical nature protecting the ship, something positively Trouserous. As soon as they passed the debris area it would be planets that they had to dodge, they were all pretty zombied and could have become dangerous had it not been for the immaculate radar system that steered them away from anything dangerous and immediately put the ship back on course once the obstacle was behind them.

Back in the entertainments room, Rodney Shook had put on his tight plastic trousers and white silk shirt and had taken the stage, together with the Biro Sisters, both wearing their silver biro suits, and a full rock band of

self-playing instruments. It was getting pretty wild. Rodney Shook's eyes came out like organ stops and matched his snow-white afro hairdo. His face, under the strange lighting, was a delicate shade of yellow ochre. He was right out of his mind on God knows what, and singing a slow instant blues called, 'This ship is gonna take me home'. It went something like this:

'This ship is gonna take me home
but I don't know where I'm goin'.
Neat Vampires at Half Price,
(Apply Within) – yeeaah.
Gimme love. uh! Gimme hope, uh!
Let me roam.
This ship – is gonna take me home.

Now let me hear it from the Biros, shake it baaabyy . . .'
The Biro Sisters began:
Shoop de wadda wop
Shoop de wadda wop
Shoop shoop de wadda wop
Ah ah ah ah . . .

It really had feeling, and wherever in the universe this dubious mission ended up, there would always be a place for talent like this, even Trouser admitted nearly being brought to tears by the emotional content of Rodney Shook's act.

They all slept soundly that night in their coloured beds and when morning came, Venus was clearly visible on the video screens as a greyish red blob set in the blackness of space. Mr Bizarre was wearing a sharp antique newspaper suit, the type that nearly caught on down the now non-existent Kings Road in the roaring 60s; and a large pink bowler hat with matching sunglasses and moustache. He stared wide-eyed at the fast approaching planet. T.G. Trouser joined him, dressed in a white nightdress and pale blue bathing cap.

'Not a pretty sight,' said Trouser, staring sleepily at the screen. 'We could touch down, if you'll pardon the expression, and check it out. What do you think, Bizer?'

Mr Bizarre answered in his deep elegant voice. 'Is there any room down there, do we need any shrinking liquid to fit in?'

'Come, come now, Bizer. It's not all that bad, I think it's only one side of the planet that's completely covered with waste materials. This side's virtually clear if we watch our step, see those reddish spots, there?' Trouser pointed at the screen.

'You mean, the ones that look like mutant blood vessels?' said Bizer.

Trouser rubbed his red chin. 'Well, personally I think they look more like wildly exaggerated pomegranate pips; but that's a matter of opinion, I suppose. Anyway . . . you get the general picture?'

'Roger,' said Bizer.

'We can land on one of those red spots and, with any luck, entirely avoid crippling Neat Vampires at Half Price (apply within). Understand? Oh, we may hit a few thousand tons of surplus ties or suspender belts and whathaveyou but we won't get badly entangled with anything too heavy. I believe the White House and that sort of stuff is on the other side. It's worth the risk, I'll take her down.'

They all agreed Venus would be worth taking a look at, except of course the pornographic Scotsman Duffy Wigman. He said it was too hazardous to chance it and that Trouser was a fool.

Trouser agreed with him and took her down. They didn't stay long, just an hour or two for a quick browse around the surplus materials. There was so much junk on Venus it was quite remarkable. It had mostly been sent up from America when the dolphins emerged although there was quite a bit of England lying around there, including the whole of Carnaby Street and its entire contents. It bloated through the back of a waste disposal module like a giant turd from a caterpillar. Most of Wigan was up there too, and Buckingham Palace. The Trouser party picked up a few old souvenirs and quickly lifted off, there was no point in hanging around on a rubbish tip, even though the turf from Wembley Stadium was taking quite nicely.

It was a relief for Trouser to see that everyone was settling in quite comfortably and adapting to the new environment they had been hurled into. Still uncertain as to their actual destination, he thought it best not to think too much about it and just let Fate take over; it was obviously a capable ship and with all the recent flying saucer sightings back on earth, he felt sure they would run into something sooner or later. He set the ship on course for the monster planet of earth's solar system, Jupiter. Meanwhile, he would busy himself interviewing the crew and writing down their comments and state of health in a big log book Hatpin Degenovitch had provided.

This was a typical day's contents.

November 18th, 2073.

Woke up.
Dressed in pin stripe dungarees and mountaineer's hat.
Put on stereo.
Made coffee.
Interviewed the seal-being, Bruce.
Bruce is looking more and more human every day.
Bruce says he wants to be an actor when fully skinned.
Interviewed platonic Englishman, Mr Straightly.
Says he would like Aunti Paperclip informed of his whereabouts.
Am getting him to rest as much as possible.
Just spoke to Kurly Krishna the Kellogg Kid via ship's radio.
He put us into total anti-fruit laugh-out.
Convulsed whole ship for a solid hour.
Dilly, the younger member of the Biro Sisters, is pregnant.
Dolse is the father. Condition, steady.
A OK.
Excuse me. Must have quick piss.

Right. Where were we?
Interviewed Mr Bizarre.
He said, 'Nothing.'
Duffy Wigman, although pessimistic about mission, has been tower of strength and fortitude, etc.
Says he will deliver Dil's baby for a small fee. His usual pubic sample.
Consumed Pen-o-bip.
Must close now.
Have set course for Jupiter, the biggy.
Venus is played out now. Will probably just miss Jupiter by a fraction.
Can't see any point in landing.
Must press on.
Over and out. Roger. A OK.

T.G. TROUSER

They all crowded around the video screens for a good look as the ship cruised over the surface of Jupiter. It was a massive planet with great purple mountains and thick patches of green clouds hundreds of miles long. Trouser shot a few of his flags down the waste disposal chute to mark their visit but it was useless to even consider landing. The planet had no breatheable atmosphere and was prone to extreme temperature changes, and its surface looked too unstable for a ship to land on. It could have been soft dust miles and miles deep between those mountains. They must head for the stars. Trouser put the ship on full speed and made radio contact.

'Hello . . . hello. Is there anybody there, Degenovitch?'

He sat in a steel tubed swivel chair, wearing an outsize cotton shirt, baggy grey trousers with an old false leather belt thrown around them, and a transparent ten gallon hat. Holding the microphone very close to his mouth, he tried again to make contact with earth.

''Ello . . . 'ello. This is Trouser speaking from Neat Vampires at Half Price (apply within), just passing Jupiter. Is that earth on the line, or just a mirage?'

There was a fast crackle and they they heard the Russian Degenovitch speaking. 'This is planet earth; Degenovitch speaking. Can't hear you too vell . . . where did you say you vere?'

'Jupiter,' answered Trouser. 'Jupiter – a great ball of nitrous gases, poisonous glaciers, giant hostile cartons of yoghourt, monstrous caterpillars with rubber jaws big enough to crush a man. Armies of swaggering Siamese twin bee-ants, ravaging all in their path. Ghastly alien forms of strange unaccountable dimension and structure, Bif Jones impersonators ray gunning renegade mutant daffodils. Craters crammed full with the rotting carcasses of surplus leather glove beings, and the mosquitoes . . . God, the mosquitoes!'

He was exaggerating slightly.

'Glad to hear you haf escaped largely unscathed, Mr Trouser,' said Degenovitch blankly. 'How is the ship going?'

'Like a rocket, Degenovitch, absolutely,' shouted Trouser, glancing at the video and seeing Jupiter dropping away from them slowly. 'We're on our way to the outer reaches, Jupiter is for the birds. We want to hit the milky ways, Andromeda even. We're going to hobnob with the dwarf stars, savvy?'

'Good, good, good,' said Degenovitch, his voice growing even fainter. 'I think we vill lose all radio contact soon so I vill quickly vish you all good luck and a happy new year. I do hope your supplies vill last out, it would be disastrous if you ran out of food and drugs.'

Trouser looked around him at the others who listened quietly. 'No, don't think there's much chance of running out of drugs. As for food . . . we have each other if worse comes to worse. It could be the next phase perhaps . . . anyway, piss off, I want to make a trunk call to Wapping. How's earth by the way, still jogging along nicely?'

'Earth is hanging on by the skin of its teeth, Mr Trouser. Exploding men haf doubled in the last year, and trick strawberries are on the increase. Kurly Krishna is down with a nasty nip on the lower abdomen – how is you mental health?'

'That's debatable,' answered Trouser. 'How's your bone structure?'

But before the scientist at ground control could answer, the radio faded and was silent. Trouser got up and looked at Twiggott. 'She's dead. Radio's dead. We're really on our own now, how does it feel?'

' 'S awright by me, boss,' said Twiggott. 'I'm ready for deep space, ain't I?'

'Yes, me too, Twigg. Still, I was expecting a little more action than this,' said Trouser with disappointment. 'I was expecting at least a few laser beam attacks from hostile alien forms using jelly bodies for disguise and robot slave shows of force and all that. Or even small green men with bulbous eyes clinging to the sides of the vessel in a futile attempt to infiltrate via the sewage disposal system. I mean, there's not even another ship about, look!' He pointed swiftly at the video and then returned his attention to Twiggott, who was wearing a tight plastic Swift Morgan space number with a false ray gun strapped around his waist, all in cool electric blue and gold.

'Jumpin' Jupiter,' continued Trouser. 'I mean, at least a few hundred highly advanced human-form-assuming blobs popping in and out with bland excuses about needing fuel to get back to Sirius Nine, etc. This is plain dull, plain dull. I do hope it livens up a bit.' He stalked around the control room adjusting the see-through ten gallon hat and fidgeting generally in impatience.

'What do you think, Duffy? Like what do you think?'

'I think you're a wee bit tay fuckun hoopful, Trewser. There's nae a wee monster here,' Duffy Wigman stood with his knobbly legs apart and his hands behind his back. 'There's nae but black space. Aye, black space and desolation, brrr, the very thought makes me shudder. Och, bug-eyed monsters indeed! Why, I've seen moore bug-eyed monsters on a Saturday night at the ould folks binge up doon at the Rose n' Thistle.' He stalked off, swinging his kilt proudly.

'Well I'm ready, Trous',' said Twiggott roughly. 'If anyfing 'as a go at us, me and the boy'sers 'ull pank it up, we'll crack 'em all eggish, no rankle.'

'Thanks, Twigg,' said Trouser.

'Anyway, Andromeda may hold the surprises, we'll see. Nothing to do now but get zombied and await results. Let's all go down and watch *The Day*

Mars invaded Euston Station, it might be a good omen, friends.'

The ship ploughed on through deep space and within six months, they were peeping into the video at the Andromeda constellation. There were stars, planets, moons, comets, and gigantic clouds of gases all around them. It was a breathtaking sight, but still there was no sign of any extraterrestrial beings, and Trouser realized they must travel even farther afield. It was only when Trouser decided the fuel tanks needed re-filling that he made a ridiculous discovery. The reading on the fuel gauge indicated that they were nearly empty, but just as they emerged from a belt of gases that marked the end of Andromeda, Trouser noticed with surprise that the fuel gauge was reading full again. He scratched his curly blonde hair and decided that there must be a fault somewhere, it had been six months of perfect flight so it was hardly surprising that something would go wrong. He asked Duffy Wigman if he would check it out.

'Duffy,' he said. 'I was about to re-fill the fuel tanks, but look, it says here that we're full up, can you poke around and verify pressures and whathaveyou. I'm sure we've developed our first fault. If so, this calls for a little celebration. It may mean we're being harassed by aliens at last, I do hope so.'

He seemed quite expectant so Duffy gave everything a full going-over. He returned an hour later to Trouser who was sitting in the control room still watching the gauge.

'Well, the gauge says full. What's amiss?'

'As far as I can see, Trewser, there's nae a fault in the system, maybe yoor at fault, do ye den what ah mean?'

'Nay, I dinna ken,' mocked Trouser.

'Weel,' ventured Duffy Wigman. 'Are ye noo sure ye have nae already refuelled – I mean, ye could a done it but forgot about it. Ah noticed you've been eating those wee green capsules a lot lately. They're not for constipation ye know!'

Trouser sighed. 'Duffy, am I not The Great T.G. Trouser, Music Therapy genius and saviour of damn near half the human race?'

'Aye.'

'And I am not well versed with inner circuitry and tri-di experience; am I not Buddha on stilts; am I not the Electric Jesus, eh?'

'Aye,' said Duffy, 'but . . .'

'But nothing, Duffy, but nothing.' As Trouser spoke he blinked one eye and then another alternately.

'Do you not think that I am capable of memorizing whether or not I have refuelled the blessed ship! C'mon Duff, lay the sandwich on me, hit me where it hurts,' he put his arm across his forehead. 'Tell me you think I've flipped.'

'Well shit and shovel, Trewser!' steamed the kilted Scotsman. 'The damn fuel is reeght oop ta the brim! Aye, we're fool reeght ta the top, ye must a done it!'

Trouser looked perplexed for a moment. He spun in the steel tubed chair and looked again at the fuel gauge which still showed the needle hard against the full mark. 'I can't tumble it,' he said at last.

Mr Straightly stumbled in, checking a graph and hiccuping loudly. 'Ah . . .

THE FUEL TANKS ARE STILL READING FULL, DID YOU CHECK OUT THE SYSTEM?
AYE.... AND THERE'S NAE A FAULT....
COPYRIGHT © WILLY SMAX 1979

EXCEPT MAYBE IN YOU TREWSER!
DUFFY..... AM I NOT THE GREAT T.G.TROUSER MUSIC THERAPY GENIUS! AM I NOT BUDDHA ON STILTS THE ELECTRIC JESUS!! C'MON DUFF, LAY THE SANDWICH ON ME, DO YOU THINK I'VE FLIPPED?!!
STOP

YES!

WHAT HO CHAPS! HIC WE'VE JUST LEFT ANDROMEDA 9, I SAY, IS ANYTHING WRONG?
DUFFY THINKS I'VE RE-FUELED AND FORGOTTEN ABOUT IT
TANK

BALLY THUNDER DUFFY!! I THINK THAT'S A BIT STRONG!
TANK

GLOW
THREE POINTS!
TANK

I say chaps, we've just left Andromeda, God only knows where we're bally well off to now. Top hole ship this, what! Splice the main brace and all that, I think it could go for ever.' He looked at the two men who were deep in thought and silent. 'I . . . I say, is anything wrong?' His head stuck out on his thin veiny neck as he spoke and his weak eyes drooped almost as much as the wispy moustache hanging over his mouth.

'It seems,' said Trouser looking at Duffy. 'It seems Duffy here, respecting his judgement as much as I do, thinks that I've refuelled the tanks and forgot about it. Look!' He showed Mr Straightly the gauge.

'Bally thunder,' said Mr Straightly. 'Now look here, Duffy old fellow, I can vouch for Mr Trouser. He may forget what he doesn't need to remember, but a silly thing like a fuel gauge . . . well, I think you're being a bit . . . a bit strong, suggesting he could forget that.'

'Three points!' bellowed the buffoon Trouser, stabbing a finger upwards at the round ceiling.

'Weel, that's as may be,' said Duffy Wigman, obviously unsatisfied.

'Perverse as it may appear,' said Trouser, 'I do respect your idiot findings, Duffy. We'll just have to count how many fuel tanks are left. That's all.'

They checked them over, and found none had been used since lift-off from earth, and the same fuel tanks that were in when they left were definitely full up. Trouser grew quite excited, he was sure they were being infiltrated by mindbending aliens. He threw a celebration party as the ship continued on its course.

But the genius Trouser was wrong. The fuel tanks were full again because of a much more sinister phenomenon than hostile aliens.

After the party, which lasted for weeks, Trouser decided it was about time to check their progress. It had been totally ignored and still there was no sign of anything positive happening. Trouser stumbled out of the relaxation room wearing a yellow party hat and holding a half empty bottle of champagne, drooping from his hand. A heavy green suit clung to him stickily, and the spotted massive bow tie around his neck appeared to be holding his head on. He hummed 'Sister Morphine' languidly as he rolled slowly along the cool slim corridor of the space ship towards the main control room, carefully stepping over Mr Straightly who had fallen asleep peacefully in the corridor.

When Trouser reached the silent control room, Twiggott and One'ser were already there standing in front of the video screens. On two of the screens the view from the back of the ship was shown. Nothing but stars, twinkling in the blackness. On another four screens, there was the view from the ship's sides. The same thing could be seen here, just stars and odd broken satellites and moons. But on the screens which showed what was happening in front of them, there was a large greyish red planet, still far away, but at this speed they would soon be upon it. Trouser silently leaned on Twiggott's shoulder and looked at the picture. He looked at Twiggott's ear as he spoke.

'Looks interesting,' he yawned and rubbed his eyes, then slugged on the bottle. 'What do you make of it, Twigg? Looks a big place to me. Is it an unknown body or what?' He staggered off and checked the graphs and electric

progress maps. 'Hum hum ho he ho hum bum bum. What the pank!' Startled, he looked up at Twiggott who grinned sardonically and chewed Pen-o-bip gum.

'I don't know what gives, boss, do I? But dere's somefing funny 'appenin' 'ere. To all accounts like, I mean, accordin' to da graphs and stuff,' he pointed a straight finger at the screens. 'Dat big planet out there, das Jupiter! Somebody's bleedin' screwed dis one up, int they?'

On hearing this, Trouser pulled his red face into a curious grimace. He rushed up to the screen and stared hard at the big planet. 'We've been cuckolded,' he said at last.

Twiggott scratched his neck. 'Uh, don't know whatcher mean, boss.'

'Duped,' said Trouser. 'Blind alleyed, turned around, surely.'

'Naw, Trous, look at the course progress chart and stuff! You 'ave a look, we ain't moved from the original course, 'ave we? I'll go an' get Duffy, 'e'll know was happenin'.

Twiggott sent One'ser off to find the Scotsman, he was still trying to find his bearings in the relaxation room after the party. Groaning, Duffy checked the charts and relevant equipment, and assured Trouser that they were still on the original course. By this time Bruce had joined them. Trouser lit a blue cigar and studied the planet on the video.

'What do you make of it, Duffy? It's Jupiter, you know, of that there's no doubt.'

'Weel, perhaps there's two Jupiters, Trouser, but I know there's been nae faults with the automatic pilot, we're still on course.'

Duffy looked over at Bruce and studied his clothes. He was wearing a dark crumpled suit with a thick navy blue polo neck pullover. Trouser looked at Duffy and followed his eyes to Bruce who spoke, staring into the screen.

'I'll be glad to get 'ome meself,' he said. 'I don't know as I understand quite what's happening up here. Mr Straightly's out of his bloody brain. I think yer all berks, all bloody daft.'

Trouser had involuntarily jerked back when he saw Bruce. He saw that his whiskers had almost entirely disappeared and his skin had lost its shiny fish-like appearance. It was sort of mottled, as if he were shedding his old skin and a new layer was coming through underneath. His head was more defined in shape now too. Trouser thought he resembled a twentieth century politician he had heard about once and seen pictures of, the man who decided to swim the Atlantic Ocean at the age of 98; What was his name now? Trouser searched his mind but could find no answer. Whoever he was, he never returned form that swim, Trouser remembered.

'Hmm, good to see you're shaping up to your new role nicely at last, Bruce. What do you make of this dilemma?'

'Eah ah don't know mate.' He still had his Northern accent though. 'Ah don't know at all. All I know is that I'd like to get back on earth again. I want to rob a bank and live in Uganda wiv a big sexy Negress.' He was still a maniac.

'Yes quite, quite,' said Trouser, uninterested now as his thoughts turned back to the problem in hand.

'What I'm worried about is . . .' He was interrupted by the red light on the radio receiver which started to flash.

'Holy constellations!' gasped T.G. Trouser, spitting the cigar out of his red lips. 'What the sponk can this mean? Marauding aliens at last? Chronic radiation freaks with perverse sexual habits and telescopic probiscusis? Or is it . . . just someone on the radio?'

'Err . . . shall I answer it?' said Bruce. 'It could be the bloody milkman.'

Trouser picked it up and spoke in a clear clipped voice. 'Hello, hello. This is the earth mission aboard Neat Vampires at Half Price (apply within). Who is trying to make contact? Repeat, Who is on the line, over.'

'Trouser!' said the voice faintly through the crackling. It was unmistakable. 'Trouser, this is Degenovitch speaking from Javaal control. Vot is happening? You should be goingk in the other direction. I haf been following your course most carefully, don't know how you are doing this!'

'It's a mystery to me too,' said Trouser. 'According to our calculations, we are still supposed to be heading away from earth. But there's no doubt that Jupiter's on our screen, we're on our way back.'

'Yes,' said Hatpin. 'You seemed to go beyond the limits of our telescope and at that point you vere . . . vell, I don't know any more than you, Mr Trouser, I don't understand what is happening, what are you goink to do, are you goingk to turn around, or what?'

Suddenly Trouser was laughing. He looked up at Jupiter, now almost filling the screen and chuckled. 'What a sandwich experience!' he bellowed. 'Degenovitch. What a slithered pincer, ha! See you on Earth, buddy. See you soon!'

He put the radio mike carefuly back on its clip and looked up at the others with a secret joke on his face. They looked back at him expectantly, waiting patiently for an answer. He raised his arms in the air.

'Okay, all of you; go down to the rest room and take your Holidays, set me up with a large scotch, and I'll explain everything. I think I have the answer–if answer it can be called.

Chapter 19
Trick

In just under a year, the space ship, Neat Vampires at Half Price (apply within), touched down on the charred plain in the mountains of Javaal. The ship stood silently as it had done once before. The sun was still hot and a sticky haze lifted from the ground. The pine trees and mountains surrounding the plain were silent and expectant. Across the blackened ground a green and yellow moped, licence number TIS 173D, picked its way, droning like a bee and carrying the Russian, Hatpin Degenovitch, towards the space ship. He was wearing a blue Italian suit with green socks and natty brown suede shoes. On his head perched a white crash helmet, and a pair of black goggles covered his eyes.

Degenovitch reached the ship and took off the helmet, forgetting the goggles. He undid his jacket buttons and switched off the moped. Then he combed his black greasy hair and stood under the ship's legs, intently waiting for the hatch to open. It opened silently high above him and a square object slipped out and telescoped down to the ground. It was the ship's silver ladder.

The first out were the Large Squad, One'ser and Two'ser, dressed in yellow banana suits and mock astros; Three'ser, Four'ser and Five'ser in white satin suits with conical wizard's hats and blue hair. Twiggott followed them in a green and red skin-tight stenolin two-piece with a purple rubber snake for a tie, humo-plastic foot-shaped boots, and his green mohican hair on the wrong way. Then came Mr Bizzare in a long white robe and curly mandarin's shoes; he looked frail and wise as he cautiously descended the ladder. Mr Straightly was next in his white hunter's hat, faded cotton shirt, beige shorts and brown plimsolls, closely followed by Duffy Wigman in his kilt and giant sporran. Then Rodney Shook and the Biro Sisters emerged. Dily was about eight months pregnant by now and waddled very carefully down the ladder with much help from the doting father, Dolse. They had to be careful. It was going to be quite an event when the baby was born, they were expecting something remarkably out of the ordinary. Finally Bruce popped out of the hatch in suedette flared trousers and a floppy vest with flags of the world printed on it. And Trouser came out last in a thick silver spacesuit, holding its large helmet in one hand.

Degenovitch greeted them with handshakes and smiles and then confronted Trouser. Trouser was unusually quiet; it was obvious he was still assessing the situation. He glanced at Degenovitch cautiously, then returned his gaze to the ground. The others wandered around or sat down nearby on the blackened ground. The Russian sucked his teeth for a moment before speaking. 'The astronauts, they are still . . . out there,' he pointed to the belt of pine trees behind the ship. 'They still vill not come to us. I thought perhaps you may haf some inkling as to what has caused them to act so strangely.'

'Inkling?' said Trouser curiously. 'Yes, that word fits,' and he looked up at the sky for a brief moment. His hair was almost a perfect reflection of the sunlight but he looked a little more flaccid than usual: he was apt to change quite suddenly, though.

'What I have to say, Degenovitch, may strike you like a haddock in a thunderstorm. Like a ton of lemons in a swimming pool.' But before the Great T.G. Trouser could continue, a strange sound reached his ears. Degenovitch's face dropped a mile. Bouncing toward them over a few old rocks and bits of scrub was a very small ball shaped object. It looked red in colour and made a grating 'pinggg' noise as it bounded along. The others had noticed it by now and were looking at Degenovitch expectantly. 'Run for it!' he shouted. 'Quick, get behind me, it's a joke strawberry!'

'Ballygad!' said Mr Straightly as they got behind Degenovitch, who had swiftly run to his moped and, out of its saddlebag, produced a small Woolworths cricket bat. Trouser, however, did not move but watched the progress of the strawberry as it hurtled closer and closer toward them. He could see its tiny teeth gnashing fiercely and small depressions appeared in the black sand as it bounded in a sinister crisscross pattern.

'Trouser, please get out of my way!' yelled Degenovitch, rushing to his side, wielding the bat. 'These bastards bite like hell, a man could lose a limb!'

Trouser continued to be unmoved, although he was obviously interested in the trick fruit. Its mode of propulsion fascinated him. 'You know, Degenovitch, we could learn a lot from these little buggers. Just look at that thing go, wow!'

Degenovitch did not answer but swung the cricket bat behind his head ready for a strike. The joke strawberry bounced deceptively slowly as it seemed to notice the opposition, then it sprang powerfully, straight towards Degenovitch. But before the scientist could swot it, Trouser stuck his right arm out straight and knocked the man over, then opening his mouth, jumped right into

the line of fire and caught the strawberry cleanly between his small teeth. Everyone cheered and looked at Trouser as he stood grinning, holding the still buzzing strawberry in his mouth.

'Vell done, Mr Trouser, you are indeed a genius!' said Degenovitch. 'Oh, they are edible, you know. It's just catching them that proves so dangerous.'

Trouser gave Degenovitch an understanding nod and then swallowed the strawberry. 'Um, not bad', said Trouser smacking his lips. 'Not bad at all, but personally I prefer gooseberries in ant sauce.'

The Russian returned the cricket bat to his saddlebag and rummaged around until he found a long thin brown cigarette. He lit it with an imitation gold lighter and returned to Trouser, pulling gently on the cigarette. He studied Trouser's face, then spoke slowly. 'Mr Trouser. You haf been gone just under a year. The ship has served you well, no?'

'No complaints,' said Trouser. 'It's a fine piece of zinc.'

'What happened?' said Degenovitch flatly. 'What secrets haf you discovered? I can tell by your face that all is not as it appears. What is the outer universe really like, why are you back on earth so soon?'

'We're not exactly back on earth, Degenovitch. Well, we are . . . and we aren't.'

Degenovitch looked baffled.

'You see, Hatpin,' continued Trouser. 'There is no universe. At least, not in the way we have previously believed it to be.'

'What do you mean?'

Trouser pointed upwards as he spoke. 'If you take a space ship into space, in any direction, you can only go as far as the most distant stars visible on our telescopes. Then, you start coming back. Oh, not to the same point in time and space, but to an exact reflection. You see, as soon as we reached the point of return, as it were, an exact mirror image of ourselves and the ship split away from us and returned to the earth that we first started from. That's why our fuel gauge suddenly read full again when it was nearly empty. That's why we didn't seem to actually have turned around when you picked up our signal again. We hadn't turned around, we'd just kept on going. Degenovitch, you are not the same Degenovitch we knew when we departed, neither are we the same people you knew. We are a mirror image. A perfect double act.'

The Russian looked a little stunned, his hands were shaking. The others were silent and neither looked too closely at each other. 'This is indeed a major breakthrough,' he said nervously. 'Are you sure? But how many . . .'

'Infinity,' interrupted Trouser. 'It is nothing but an infinite crystal ball, each facet reflects the one next to it perfectly.' He pointed to his head. 'It's not only inside, it's outside too.' He scuffled his feet in the black sand. 'Trick,' he said ironically. 'It's just a trick.'

Degenovitch let out an involuntary gasp as the full implications of the matter hit him. Trouser changed the subject, so did the infinite other Trousers on the infinite other earths.

'How's Kurly Krishna, by the way? Still out of action?'

'Krishna?' said the infinity of Degenovitch's. 'Yes . . . yes, he's been out since the first attack but he went back in again almost immediately.'

'Oh?' said Trouser.

'Er, yes . . . he got into a tangle with a hostile melon . . .' his voice dropped away quietly and he glanced at Trouser as if for reassurance. 'B . . . but Mr Trouser. Where is the real me?'

'The what?' boomed Trouser. 'You must be kidding, Hatpin, old chum, ha, you must be kidding!'

'The astronauts then, what happened there?'

'Christ knows,' said Trouser, still scuffling his silver space boots in the black sand. 'They've been travelling for years. God knows where they started from.'

'I see . . .' said the Russian. 'Then what you going to do, Trouser? What is any of us going to do?'

'Well, I've already spoken to the others. They're staying here. One earth's as good as another, it makes no difference. As for me . . .' He looked up at the blue sky. ''I'm going up again. I'm going to find the way out.'

'Do you think there is a vay out?' said Degenovitch.

'Oh, there must be. There's the big bugger with the pen for a start, understand?'

He didn't.

Trouser left Degenovitch staring dumbly into space as he shook hands with his friends. 'I'll miss you all. But no doubt we'll collide again somewhere.'

They were all very sad to part with him, but none wanted to take the chance and leave the ground again. It was definitely Trouser's trip now. He walked back to Degenovitch and patted him on the shoulder, then stripped off the space suit to reveal a cotton Hawaiian shirt and sky blue gym shorts. He lit a pink cigar, then turning on his heel walked casually towards the space ship singing Bobby Vee's 'Rubber Ball'. 'Bouncy, bouncy, bouncy, bouncy.'

As Trouser climbed the ladder up to the hatch, both Mr Straightly and Bruce were sure they noticed two slight lumps just between his shoulder blades. Whether wings would be of any use to him he would doubtless find out for himself. He blasted off.